Vocabulary for Success

COURSE I

HAROLD LEVINE
Chairman Emeritus of English,
Benjamin Cardozo High School, New York

NORMAN LEVINE
Associate Professor of English,
City College of the City University of New York

ROBERT T. LEVINE
Professor of English,
North Carolina A & T State University

AMSCO

AMSCO SCHOOL PUBLICATIONS, INC.
315 Hudson Street / New York, N.Y. 10013

Vocabulary books by the authors

Vocabulary and Composition Through Pleasurable Reading,
Books I–IV
Vocabulary for Enjoyment, Books I–III
Vocabulary for the High School Student, Books A, B
Vocabulary for the High School Student
Vocabulary for the College-Bound Student
The Joy of Vocabulary
Vocabulary for Success, Courses I–IV

Contributing Writer: Steven L. Stern
Cover Design: Meghan J. Shupe
Composition: Brad Walrod/High Text Graphics, Inc.

Please visit our Web site at:
www.amscopub.com

When ordering this book, please specify
either **R 011 P** or VOCABULARY FOR SUCCESS, COURSE I

ISBN 1-56765-129-1
NYC Item 56765-129-0

To the Student

Vocabulary for Success, Course I teaches not only words but skills—especially the skills of close reading, critical thinking, and concise writing.

Every time you meet a lesson word in this book, you will be called upon to complete a sentence—not with the lesson word but with some other missing word. This, though you may not think so at first, requires close reading and critical thinking. Try to do what you are asked to do on page 1, and see if you don't agree. Then, for an example of a different way in which the book teaches these same skills, see page 38.

Concise writing is still another skill you will be learning in every lesson in this vocabulary book. The fastest way to learn what this skill is about is to turn now to the first concise writing exercise on page 8.

By the time you finish the book, you will have had hundreds of opportunities to perfect your reading, writing, and thinking skills and you also will have learned many hundreds of useful words that belong in a well-educated person's vocabulary. Take a minute now to skim the Vocabulary Index, pages 144–149.

You will find ample provision for review within each regular lesson. Note, too, that after every fourth lesson is a unit review.

Analogy questions have been included at the end of each unit, in part because they help with the review of lesson words and their synonyms, but more importantly because they stimulate critical thinking, a principal concern of this book.

The Authors

Contents

LESSON 1

Lesson Preview

Some of the words that you will encounter on pages 1–2 and 4–5 of this lesson appear in bold type in the following poem. Read the poem, and on a separate sheet of paper, answer the questions that follow.

> I need to be **candid**, the instructor said.
> Your driving has numerous **flaws**.
> You must stay **alert** and watch other cars,
> And when the sign says Yield, you must pause!
>
> You're just a **novice**, and your life is at risk
> If you **neglect** the roadside signs.
> So obey the laws and the speed limit too,
> Or you'll pay a fortune in fines.

Who is the speaker in this poem? Who is the listener? What is this poem about?

 LESSON WORDS 1–10: Pronounce the word, spell it, study its meanings, and finish the sentence that follows it. See 1, below.

---

alert (adj.)   wide-awake and ready to act quickly; **watchful**;
ə-'lərt   **vigilant**

    1. Be *alert*; remove the pot from the stove (after, before)
       before   it boils over.

brawny (adj.)   having well-developed muscles; **muscular**; **strong**;
'brȯ-nē   **sinewy**

    2. Weight (lifters, watchers) _____ develop *brawny* shoulders.

1

candid (*adj.*)   open and honest in what one says or does; **frank**;
'kan-dəd   **outspoken**

3. *Candid* people tell the truth (except, even) _____
   when it hurts.

chide (*v.*)   express mild disapproval of; **scold**; **reprove**;
'chīd   **reproach**

4. We use (gentle, harsh) _____ tones when we *chide*
   someone.

counterfeit (*adj.*)   made to resemble something genuine with
'kaùnt-ər-,fit   intent to deceive; **forged**; **bogus**; **sham**

5. I was (heartbroken, pretending) _____; I shed
   counterfeit tears.

culprit (*n.*)   person guilty of any offense or crime; **offender**;
'kəl-,prit   **malefactor**

6. Don't (accuse, trust) _____ her; she is not the
   culprit.

defraud (*v.*)   deprive (someone) of something by deception or
di-'frȯd   fraud; **cheat**; **bilk**

7. If you were paid in (genuine, bogus) _____ money,
   you were *defrauded*.

flaw (*n.*)   something faulty or missing; **defect**; **imperfection**;
,flȯ   **blemish**

8. (Selfishness, Poverty) _____ is a serious character
   flaw.

goad (*v.*)   prod, as with a pointed stick; **spur**; **urge**; **incite**; **impel**
'gōd

9. I quit (willingly, unwillingly) _____; no one *goaded*
   me to do it.

maul (*v.*)   handle roughly; injure by beating; **batter**; **mangle**
'mól

> 10. The child's new doll was *mauled* by her (jealous, gentle)
> _____ playmates.

SENTENCE COMPLETION 1–10: Enter the required lesson
words, as in 1, below.

---

1. The defendants ____**defraud**____ ed people of millions of dollars
   by printing and circulating __**counterfeit**__ bills.

2. If you had been more _____, you would have noticed
   the _____ in the merchandise before purchasing it.

3. At first, he was not _____ with us, but by gentle urging,
   and appealing to his better nature, we _____**ed** him
   into telling the truth.

4. The _____ champion _____**ed** the challenger
   so badly that the referee had to stop the bout.

5. Since the _____**s** had committed a serious offense, they
   should have been punished, instead of just being _____
   ed.

VOCABULARY IN CONTEXT 1–10: Read the paragraph,
and on a separate sheet of paper, answer the questions
that follow. Do not repeat any of the underlined words in
your answers; use synonyms instead.

Computer users must be <u>alert</u> when using the Internet. Unfortu-
nately, there are many people ready to <u>defraud</u> the unsuspect-
ing user. There are even <u>counterfeit</u> Web sites designed to trick
users into revealing personal information. These Web sites,
nearly identical with the true sites, are used by criminals to steal
social security numbers, passwords, and charge card numbers.

1. What is the main idea of this paragraph?

2. Suppose the police catch the creator of a counterfeit Web site. What do you think would be an appropriate punishment for the culprit?

LESSON WORDS 11–20: Pronounce the word, spell it, study its meanings, and finish the sentence that follows it.

---

neglect (v.)   give little or no attention to; **disregard**; **ignore**
ni -'glekt

11. A *neglected* room looks (untidy, neat) _____.

novice (n.)   person new at something; **beginner**; **apprentice**;
'nä-vəs   **neophyte**; **tyro**

12. It is (rare, normal) _____ for *novices* to make mistakes.

obstinate (adj.)   unyielding; unreasonably determined to have
'äb-stə-nət   one's way; **stubborn**; **intransigent**

13. *Obstinate* people (seldom, often) _____ change their views.

peer (n.)   person of the same standing or ability as another; **equal**;
'pir   **match**

14. Pat is Jim's *peer* in tennis, but in other sports there is (little, considerable) _____ difference between them.

proficient (adj.)   highly competent; **skilled**; **adept**
prə-'fi-shənt

15. Chris is *proficient* with a needle, but I (can, can't) _____ sew.

prohibit (v.)   forbid by law or order; **ban**; **outlaw**; **interdict**
prō-'hi-bət

16. Selling (soft, alcoholic) _____ drinks to children is *prohibited*.

sleuth (*n.*)   one who follows a track or clue; **bloodhound**;
 'slüth   **detective**; **investigator**

   17. The arrests were made by *sleuths* posing as (addicts, police)
       _____.

truce (*n.*)   temporary cessation of fighting; **cease-fire**; **armistice**
 'trüs

   18. Casualties went (up, down) _____ considerably
       during the *truce*.

wan (*adj.*)   pale, as from sickness or anxiety; **ashen**; **pallid**
 'wän

   19. You look *wan*. Is something (amusing, worrying)
       _____ you?

wrath (*n.*)   intense anger; resentful indignation; **ire**; **rage**; **fury**
 'rath

   20. (Wise, Quick) _____ decisions are rarely made in
       moments of *wrath*.

SENTENCE COMPLETION 11–20: Enter the required
lesson words from D, above.

---

 1. Both sides are _____**ed** from moving reinforcements
    into the battle zone during the _____.

 2. As a(n) _____, Sherlock Holmes was in a class by him-
    self; he had no _____.

 3. _____**s** in carpentry are not expected to be
    _____ with tools.

 4. Her friend has been _____**ing** his health; he looks
    _____.

 5. Their _____ refusal to compromise has aroused our
    _____.

VOCABULARY IN CONTEXT 11–20: Read the paragraph, and on a separate sheet of paper, answer the questions that follow. Do not repeat any of the underlined words in your answers; use synonyms instead.

Jacques Moreau was widely regarded as the most brilliant <u>sleuth</u> in all of France. Madeleine, his assistant, was <u>proficient</u>, but no one regarded her as Moreau's <u>peer</u>. After all, she was little more than a <u>novice</u>. Imagine the people's surprise when they heard the news. It was young Madeleine, not the great Moreau, who had solved the Bank of Paris robbery!

1. What is the main idea of this paragraph?

2. If you were Jacques Moreau, would the news cause you to react with <u>wrath</u>? Why or why not?

SYNONYMS: To avoid repetition, replace the boldfaced word or expression with a synonym from the vocabulary list below. See 1, below.

batter	malefactor	bilk	vigilant	tyro
armistice	defect	intransigent	adept	reproach

1. The fighting ceased when the
   cease-fire was agreed to.   1. ____armistice____

2. She was **unyielding**; she wouldn't
   yield an inch.   2. _____

3. We were in a state of alertness;
   everyone was told to be **alert**.   3. _____

4. Who is the **offender** who committed
   these offenses?   4. _____

5. Sometimes a **beginner** does well
   from the very beginning.   5. _____

6. Those thugs are rough; they
   rough up their victims.   6. _____

7. He lacks proficiency in typing; he is not as **proficient** as you.

7. _____

8. She lifted a chiding finger, as if to **chide** us.

8. _____

9. Don't let those frauds **defraud** you.

9. _____

10. The gloves marked "imperfect" have a slight **imperfection**.

10. _____

 ANTONYMS: In the blank space in each sentence below, enter the word most nearly the antonym of the boldfaced word or words. Choose your antonyms from the following list. See 1, below.

---

adept	sinewy	bogus	ignore	outspoken
ban	stubborn	neophyte	ashen	reprove

1. Every **veteran** in golf was once a(n) __neophyte__.

2. We **commend** those who excel and _____ those who loaf.

3. An expert can distinguish a(n) _____ diamond from a **genuine** one.

4. Many **give a great deal of attention** to TV but _____ their studies.

5. The rules _____ campfires but **permit** hiking.

6. The _____ stranger helped **frail** fellow passengers with their luggage.

7. Doesn't a(n) _____ employee deserve more pay than an **incompetent** one?

8. Most were **easy to persuade**, but one _____ member refused to cooperate.

9. They are usually _____, but this time they were **not candid** with us.

10. The patient who was _____ a week ago now looks much more **healthy**.

CONCISE WRITING: Express the thought of each sentence in NO MORE THAN FOUR WORDS. See 1, below.

1. The people who lived next door to us were unreasonably determined to have their own way.

   Our neighbors were obstinate.

2. We paid too little attention to the employees who were new to the job.

   _____

3. The mechanic that she has been using is highly competent.

   _____

4. Not too many people in this wide world are open and honest in what they say and do.

   _____

5. He had the pale look of someone who is ill or extremely worried about something.

   _____

6. It is essential for guards to be watchful and ready to act quickly.

   _____

7. You are a person of the same ability as myself.

   _____

8. The smoking of cigarettes or cigars is forbidden by law in this building.

   _____

VOCABULARY SKILL BUILDER

J

Context Clues: Descriptive Information

You can often figure out the meaning of an unfamiliar word from its context. *Context* means the surrounding words or sentences.

Clues in the context take many different forms. For example, the context may include descriptive details that suggest the meaning of an unfamiliar word.

Example: We were shocked to see Jason's <u>wan</u> face. He looked so pale and thin that we were sure he was ill.

Context clues: "So pale and thin that we were sure he was ill" describes Jason's *wan* appearance.

Example: "You are the most <u>obstinate</u> person I've ever met," she cried. "You always have to have things your way, and you refuse to compromise!"

Context clues: The phrases "always have to have things your way" and "refuse to compromise" describe what it means to be an *obstinate* person.

Exercises

Circle context clues that can help you figure out the meaning of the underlined word.

1. Davis was a large man with a <u>brawny</u> build, who could lift 100 pounds with no effort.

2. Vanna is the best watchdog I've ever had. She's always <u>alert</u>, listening to every sound, ready to spring into action.

3. New school rules <u>prohibit</u> inappropriate clothing. Any student who comes to class wearing torn or ragged jeans or a T-shirt displaying offensive words will be sent home to change.

WRITING SKILL BUILDER

Stating and Supporting a Position

Some writing assignments ask you to take a position on an issue. You will usually find it helpful to state your position in a topic sentence. Writing a topic sentence focuses your writing and prepares readers for what follows.

Once you have stated your position in a topic sentence, you have to support that position with information. Supporting information should include specific reasons, facts, or examples. It is not enough just to say that you think a certain way. You have to back up your point of view with specific reasons *why* you think as you do.

Activity

Some educators say that students are required to take too many tests. Others insist that the tests that students take are necessary to measure their learning. What is your view?

On a separate sheet of paper, write a topic sentence expressing your viewpoint about this issue. Then write three sentences that support your position with specific reasons, facts, or examples. In your sentences, use at least two of the words that you have learned in this lesson.

LESSON 2

Some of the words that you will encounter on pages 11–12 and 14–15 of this lesson appear in bold type in the following paragraph.

> Last summer was one of the hottest and driest on record. Day after day, the sun's burning rays **parched** the ground. There was such a **dearth** of rain that the soil cracked and the grass **wilted**. Fields and meadows lost their bright colors as flowers became **sparse**.

In Lesson 1's *Vocabulary Skill Builder*, you learned how descriptive information in context clues can suggest the meaning of unfamiliar words. What descriptive details help you understand what this paragraph is about? Write your answer on a separate sheet of paper.

 LESSON WORDS 1–10: Pronounce the word, spell it, study its meanings, and finish the sentence that follows it. See 1, below.

---

antagonistic (*adj.*)   showing opposition or ill will; **opposed**;
(,)an-,ta-gǝ-'nis-tik   **hostile; inimical**

    1. My (friends, foes) ____**friends**____ were unexpectedly *antagonistic* to my idea.

botch (*v.*)   do clumsily; spoil by poor work; foul up; **bungle; ruin**
'bäch

    2. A (careful, careless) _____ mechanic *botched* the repair job.

dearth (*n.*)   inadequate supply; **scarcity; lack**
'dǝrth

    3. Homes were (easy, hard) _____ to find; there was a *dearth* of housing.

dire (*adj.*)   arousing dread or deep distress; **dreadful**; **ominous**;
ˈdīr   **threatening**

> 4. We heard the *dire* forecast of the (end, spread)
>   _____ of democracy.

dolt (*n.*)   dull, stupid person; **dunce**; **oaf**; **clod**; **blockhead**
ˈdōlt

> 5. When I forget my (keys, fears) _____, I feel like a
>   *dolt*.

fraught (*adj.*)   full of (followed by *with*); **filled**; **laden**; **charged**
ˈfrȯt

> 6. (Familiar, New) _____ ventures are often *fraught*
>   with surprises.

glut (*n.*)   supply that exceeds demand; **oversupply**; **surplus**;
ˈglət   **superabundance**

> 7. Dealers (enjoy, dislike) _____ having a *glut* of new
>   merchandise.

humane (*adj.*)   full of sympathy and consideration for others and
hyü-ˈmān   for animals; **charitable**; **altruistic**

> 8. *Humane* people try to (ease, ignore) _____ the suf-
>   fering of others.

intrude (*v.*)   thrust oneself without invitation; **encroach**; **trespass**
in-ˈtrüd

> 9. It is very rude to *intrude* in a (private, public)
>   _____ discussion.

loath (*adj.*)   strongly disinclined; **unwilling**; **reluctant**; **hesitant**
ˈlōth

> 10. People are *loath* to part with something they (dislike, need)
>   _____.

SENTENCE COMPLETION 1–10: Enter the required lesson words.

1. Everyone was _____ to the hungry ex-convict, except one _____ bishop, who invited him to dinner and gave him a lodging for the night.

2. I felt like a(n) _____ when I _____**ed** a simple arithmetic problem.

3. Holmes was _____ to ask Watson to join him on the mission because it was _____ with danger.

4. When there was a(n) _____ of tomatoes, they were $3.00 a pound; now that there is a(n) _____ of tomatoes, they are three pounds for $1.00.

5. Ignoring _____ warnings from the townspeople, the hero and heroine went ahead with their plan to _____ on Count Dracula's privacy.

VOCABULARY IN CONTEXT 1–10: Read the paragraph, and on a separate sheet of paper, answer the questions that follow. Do not repeat any of the underlined words in your answers; use synonyms instead.

In the story, a fire-breathing dragon threatened to burn down the village. The frightened villagers saw no way out of their <u>dire</u> situation. Everyone was <u>loath</u> to do battle with the dragon.

"Only a <u>dolt</u> would take on such a monster," the mayor said. "Every possible solution is <u>fraught</u> with danger. We have no choice but to abandon our <u>village</u>."

1. Do you agree with the mayor's advice? Why or why not?

2. Do you think this story is suitable for young children? Give reasons for your answer.

novelty (*n.*)   something new; **newness**; **change**; **innovation**
'nä-vəl-tē

11. A (heat, cold) _____ wave at the North Pole would be a *novelty*.

parch (*v.*)   make dry with heat; **dry**; **scorch**; **dehydrate**
'pärch

12. The summer (drought, hurricane) _____ *parched* the landscape.

rue (*v.*)   wish undone; feel remorse for; **regret**; **deplore**
'rü

13. If you act (cautiously, hastily) _____, you may *rue* the outcome.

sparse (*adj.*)   thinly scattered; not dense; **meager**; **scanty**
'spärs

14. A (losing, winning) _____ team usually draws *sparse* crowds.

teem (*v.*)   be abundant; **abound**; **swarm**
'tēm

15. In (summer, winter) _____, the beaches *teem* with bathers.

tractable (*adj.*)   easy to manage or control; **compliant**; **docile**;
'trak-tə-bəl   **obedient**

16. *Tractable* pupils do not (disregard, heed) _____ instructions.

trite (*adj.*)   so overused as no longer to have interest, freshness, or
'trīt   originality; **commonplace**; **stale**; **timeworn**

> 17. A creative writer tries to (avoid, use) _____ *trite*
>   expressions.

unruly (*adj.*)   resistant to discipline or control; **ungovernable**;
ˌən-'rü-lē   **recalcitrant**

> 18. A (dull, fascinating) _____ program may make an
>   audience *unruly*.

wharf (*n.*)   structure where ships load and unload; **dock**; **pier**
'hwȯrf

> 19. The (limousine, yacht) _____ was tied up along the
>   *wharf*.

wilt (*v.*)   lose, or cause to lose, freshness and become limp; **droop**;
'wilt   **wither**

> 20. The *wilting* plants sprang to life after the (rain, frost)
>   _____ .

SENTENCE COMPLETION 11–20: Enter the required
lesson words from D, above.

---

1. The garden _____**s** with destructive beetles when the
    population of their natural enemies is _____ .

2. As the empty rowboat drifted from the shore, we
    _____**d** our carelessness in not tying the boat firmly
    to the _____ .

3. Max's dog Fido was so _____ that he was sent to obedi-
    ence school for a month; since his return, he has been more

    _____ .

4. There is not one bit of _____ in that movie; every idea,
    every situation, every word in it is _____ .

5. August's dry heat _____**ed** the soil and
    _____**ed** the corn.

VOCABULARY IN CONTEXT 11–20: Read the paragraph, and on a separate sheet of paper, answer the questions that follow. Do not repeat any of the underlined words in your answers; use synonyms instead.

Teachers had always regarded Ian as an <u>unruly</u> student, much less <u>tractable</u> than his classmates. However, his behavior changed once Ian discovered that he had writing talent. His essays were not <u>trite</u> accounts of everyday events. They were exciting works filled with <u>novelty</u>. Teachers and students alike praised his skill with words.

1. Why do you think Ian's behavior changed?

2. Many people say that TV programs are trite, with little novelty. Do you agree or disagree? Give reasons for your answer.

SYNONYMS: To avoid repetition, replace the boldfaced word or expression with a synonym from the vocabulary list below. See 1, below.

oaf	deplore	pier	wither	bungle
innovation	recalcitrant	inimical	altruistic	ominous

1. At what **dock** is the ship docked?   1. _____**pier**_____

2. People want something new; they like **newness**.   2. _____

3. The fresh-cut flowers are beginning to **lose freshness**.   3. _____

4. A few of our old friends are now **unfriendly** to us.   4. _____

5. I did not regret my part in the play, but I **regretted** my foolishness in turning down the leading role when it was offered.   5. _____**d**

6. Most of the youngsters were fairly easy to control; only a few were **resistant to control**.   6. _____

7. Some individuals show no
   consideration for others;
   they are not **considerate**.   7. _____

8. The work may be **done clumsily**
   if entrusted to clumsy hands.   8. _____**d**

9. So **dreadful** were the first reports
   of the earthquake that we dreaded
   hearing any more about it.   9. _____

10. Though you are surely not a(an)
    stupid person, you showed
    unbelievable stupidity.   10. _____

H **ANTONYMS:** In the blank space in each sentence below,
   enter the word most nearly the antonym of the boldfaced
   word or words. Choose your antonyms from the following
   list. See 1, below.

---

hesitant	timeworn	clod	encroach	abound
hostile	meager	docile	charitable	superabundance

1. This **congested** island formerly had a very ___**meager**___
   population.

2. Trespassers, **keep out**; do not _____ on this
   property.

3. There is no **dearth** of help; we have a(n) _____ of
   volunteers.

4. Did the casualties result from **friendly** or _____
   gunfire?

5. You should abandon your **inhumane** attitude and try to be

   _____.

6. Though a few are _____, most are **willing** to
   participate.

7. If opportunities **are scarce** here, seek a place where they

   _____.

8. A(n) _____ expression should be replaced with something **original**.

9. Even an **intelligent person** can sometimes behave like a(n)
_____.

10. What makes a(n) _____ child suddenly become
disobedient?

 CONCISE WRITING: Express the thought of each sentence in NO MORE THAN FOUR WORDS, as in 1, below.

---

1. The ideas that he is proposing are not new, but have been heard time and time again in the past.

   His ideas are trite.
   _____

2. These flowers are losing their freshness and are becoming limp.

   _____

3. We wish the mistakes that we have made were undone.

   _____

4. Shouldn't everyone have sympathy and consideration for other human beings?

   _____

5. The pupils that she has been teaching are not difficult to manage.

   _____

6. The management expels those who have the nerve to come to share in the festivities without being invited.

   _____

VOCABULARY SKILL BUILDER

Context Clues: Synonyms

A synonym is a word that means the same or almost the same as another word. For example, *dock* and *pier* are synonyms for *wharf*. A synonym that appears before or after an unfamiliar word can help you figure out the word's meaning. The synonym may appear in the same sentence as the unfamiliar word or in a separate sentence.

> *Example:* The two candidates were openly hostile to each other, although no one knew why they were so antagonistic.

Context clue: *Hostile* is a synonym for *antagonistic*.

> *Example:* "You will rue the day that you broke the law," said the judge. "You will regret what you have done."

Context clue: *Regret* in the second sentence is a synonym for *rue*.

Exercises

Circle the synonym that can help you figure out the meaning of the underlined word.

1. Keri is loath to borrow money from anyone and especially reluctant to accept a loan from her sister.

2. Eric botched the last repair job, and he's sure to bungle this one, too.

3. At first, the children were fascinated by the novelty of the toy. Once its newness wore off, though, they became bored with it.

WRITING SKILL BUILDER

Writing a Clear Topic Sentence

A topic sentence should clearly state a paragraph's main idea. It should not be too broad or vague.

Too broad: Watching television is a waste of time.

Better: Television has too little worthwhile content and too much advertising.

Activity

Kids have so many activities to choose from that no one should ever be bored. Do you agree or disagree with this statement? Why?

On a separate sheet of paper, write a topic sentence that clearly states your point of view. Then write three sentences that support your position with specific reasons, facts, or examples. In your sentences, use at least two of the words that you have learned in this lesson.

LESSON 3

Some of the words that you will encounter on pages 20–21 and
24–25 of this lesson appear in bold type in the following poem. Read
the poem, and on a separate sheet of paper, answer the questions
that follow.

> First, you need to establish your goals.
> Then, to achieve them, you must **persist**.
> Though there may be some who **scoff** at you,
> Feeling discouraged you must resist.
> **Devise** a plan, and try your hardest.
> Don't be **timid** about what you do.
> A **feasible** plan may bring success,
> And your lifelong dreams may come true.

What is the main idea of this poem? Do you agree with the poet's
advice? Why or why not?

 LESSON WORDS 1–10: Pronounce the word, spell it,
study its meanings, and finish the sentence that follows it.

---

abate (*v.*)   diminish in force or intensity; let up; **moderate**;
ə-′bāt   **subside**

    1. We took shelter (after, until) ＿＿＿＿＿＿＿ the storm
       abated.

cower (*v.*)   crouch in fear from something that threatens; **cringe**;
′kau̇(-ə)r   **quail**

    2. A (bully, clown) ＿＿＿＿＿＿ enjoys making others
       cower.

crest (*n.*)   highest part; **top**; **summit**
′krest

    3. Heavy trucks (lose, gain) ＿＿＿＿＿＿＿ speed approaching
       the *crest* of a road.

devise (v.)   make up; **concoct**; **formulate**; **design**
di-'vīz

    4. (Troops, Commanders) _____ generally do not
       devise battle plans.

din (n.)   steady loud noise; **uproar**; **racket**; **tumult**
'din

    5. A rumbling *din* accompanied the (fashion, fireworks)
       _____ display.

entreat (v.)   ask earnestly; plead with; **beg**; **beseech**; **implore**;
in-'trēt   **importune**

    6. We wanted to leave, but they *entreated* us to (go, stay)
      _____.

feasible (adj.)   capable of being done; **doable**; **possible**;
'fē-zə-bəl   **practicable**; **viable**

    7. Before (1776, 1492) _____, a transatlantic voyage
      was not deemed *feasible*.

groundless (adj.)   without foundation; uncalled for; **baseless**;
'graúnd-ləs   **gratuitous**

    8. Joe is (fine, ill) _____; your fears about his health
      are *groundless*.

horde (n.)   large, moving crowd; **multitude**; **throng**; **mob**
'hórd

    9. Merchants are (happy, unhappy) _____when
      hordes of tourists arrive.

loom (v.)   come into view indistinctly; take shape; **appear**;
'lüm   **emerge**

    10. A battle *looms* whenever old (friends, foes) _____
      cross paths.

SENTENCE COMPLETION 1–10: Enter the required lesson words.

1. When the horrid bulk of a dragon _____s at the cave's entrance, even the bravest knights _____.

2. Looking down from the hill's _____, Don Quixote claimed to see a(n) _____ of armed foes, but his squire Sancho Panza saw only a cloud of dust.

3. The attorney _____**ed** the jury to ignore the _____ accusations that had been leveled against her client.

4. Randy thought the plan that the committee had _____**d** would not work, but most of the other members believed it to be _____.

5. I hope the _____ that is interfering with our conversation will soon _____.

VOCABULARY IN CONTEXT 1–10: Read the paragraph, and on a separate sheet of paper, answer the questions that follow. Do not repeat any of the underlined words in your answers; use synonyms instead.

Audiences seem to enjoy horror films, no matter how unrealistic they may be. I remember one movie in which a teenager hears a strange <u>din</u> coming from the woods. She walks into this dark forest alone and unafraid. Anyone with half a brain would have <u>devised</u> a plan or <u>entreated</u> someone else to come along. But not this teen. Even when a huge monster <u>looms</u> into sight, the girl's courage does not <u>abate</u>. She refuses to <u>cower</u> in the bushes. Instead, she proceeds bravely onward—until she becomes the monster's dinner. And the audience loved it.

1. Paraphrase the paragraph. (To paraphrase a paragraph is to retell it in your own words.)

2. Does a movie have to be realistic to be enjoyable? Give reasons for your answer.

LESSON WORDS 11–20: Pronounce the word, spell it, study its meanings, and finish the sentence that follows it.

---

patron (*n.*)   regular customer; **client**; **supporter**
ˈpā-trən

    11. A business may (fail, prosper) _____ if it displeases its *patrons.*

persist (*v.*)   go on despite difficulty; refuse to give up; **persevere**;
pər-ˈsist   **continue**

    12. Some (heed, ignore) _____ all warnings and *persist* in smoking.

prone (*adj.*)   having a natural bent or tendency; **inclined**;
ˈprōn   **disposed; apt**

    13. A person who is (seldom, often) _____ wrong may be *prone* to error.

prudent (*adj.*)   showing sound judgment; **sensible**; **wise**;
ˈprü-dᵊnt   **judicious; discreet**

    14. It is *prudent* to (close, lock) _____ all doors before leaving home.

rouse (*v.*)   bring out of a state of inactivity; **wake**; **stir**; **excite**;
ˈraůz   **provoke**

    15. The (stillness, doorbell) _____ *roused* me from my daydream.

scoff (*v.*)   show scornful disapproval; **sneer**; **jeer**; **gibe**
ˈskȯf

    16. People *scoff* at those who claim to know (everything, little) _____ .

sham (*n.*)   something not what it is supposed to be; **hoax**; **fake**
ˈsham

    17. If he was (able, forbidden) _____ to testify, his trial was a *sham.*

spurn (v.)   reject disdainfully; turn down; **decline**; **refuse**; **scorn**
'spərn

    18. Workers *spurn* contracts that (reduce, raise) _____
        their earnings.

timid (adj.)   easily frightened; **afraid**; **timorous**; **shy**
'ti-məd

    19. *Timid* individuals are (disinclined, prone) _____ to
        complain.

unkempt (adj.)   not neat or orderly; **uncombed**; **disheveled**;
ˌən-'kem(p)t   **untidy**; **slovenly**

    20. We are (unlikely, disposed) _____ to be *unkempt*
        when we first awake.

 SENTENCE COMPLETION 11–20: Enter the required
lesson words from D, above.

---

1. A snake approaching a nest can _____ a normally
   _____ bird to attack fiercely.

2. Though the people in town _____ed at the idea of a fly-
   ing machine, the Wright brothers _____ed until their
   airplane worked.

3. Since my brother believed Rita was _____ to accidents,
   he graciously offered to do some or all of the driving, but she
   _____ed the offer.

4. Kenny is usually _____, but he realizes it is
   _____ to comb his hair before going to be interviewed
   for a job.

5. A store whose so-called "sales" are a(n) _____ cannot
   count on me as one of its _____**s**.

VOCABULARY IN CONTEXT 11–20: Read the paragraph, and on a separate sheet of paper, answer the questions that follow. Do not repeat any of the underlined words in your answers; use synonyms instead.

Some people insist that they are <u>prone</u> to accidents. These are the people who always seem to be tripping over objects or smashing their fingers with hammers. However, others <u>scoff</u> at the idea that anyone has a natural tendency to get hurt. They argue that such accidents are simply the result of carelessness. Watch where you are walking, they say, and be <u>prudent</u> when using a hammer, and you won't injure yourself.

1. What two viewpoints are described in this paragraph?

2. Which point of view do you agree with? Why?

SYNONYMS: To avoid repetition, replace the boldfaced word or expression with a synonym from the vocabulary list below.

multitude	viable	judicious	subside	concoct
baseless	quail	decline	implore	disheveled

1. Even when you comb unruly hair, it may look **uncombed**.

1. _____

2. The rain has not let up; we can't leave until it **lets up**.

2. _____ **s**

3. If your plan is **practicable**, we will put it into practice.

3. _____

4. They **pleaded with** us to wait, but we ignored their plea.

4. _____ **d**

5. Are there grounds for worry, or are your fears **groundless**?

5. _____

6. I am sure you have the sense to make a **sensible** choice.

6. _____

7. Their refusal surprises me; they have never **refused** our help.

7. _____ **d**

8. The place was crowded; it was hard
   to find anyone in that **crowd**.   8. _____

9. When danger looms, act quickly;
   don't **cower** like a coward.   9. _____

10. Someone has just **devised** a new
    device to combat auto theft.   10. _____**ed**

ANTONYMS: In the blank space in each sentence below, enter the word most nearly the antonym of the boldfaced word or words. Choose your antonyms from the following list.

---

tumult	discreet	moderate	summit	persevere
untidy	doable	timorous	emerge	scorn

1. As soon as one problem **disappears**, another _____**s** on the horizon.

2. Most **give up** quickly, but a few _____ until they reach their goal.

3. There is no telling whether the storm will **intensify** or _____.

4. What seems _____ on paper may be **impossible** in practice.

5. How long did it take to get to the _____ of the hill from its **base**?

6. Today we reconsidered and **embraced** a plan that we had _____**ed** only yesterday.

7. The _____ of wailing sirens shattered the **stillness** of the night.

8. Everyone at the dance was **well groomed**; no one was _____.

9. Not all were **courageous**; a few were so _____ that they fled in panic.

10. Even _____ shoppers occasionally make an **unwise** purchase.

CONCISE WRITING: Express the thought of each sentence in NO MORE THAN FOUR WORDS.

1. Is the pain that he has been suffering from diminishing in intensity?

_____

2. All of a sudden, the steady loud noise came to an end.

_____

3. There is no foundation for the accusations that she has been making.

_____

4. In all probability, I looked as if I had given little or no attention to my personal appearance.

_____

5. Ahead, the mountains were coming into view in indistinct form.

_____

6. What is it that made you refuse to give up?

_____

VOCABULARY SKILL BUILDER

Context Clues: Antonyms

An antonym is a word that has the opposite meaning of another word. For example, *prudent* and *foolish* are antonyms. An antonym that appears before or after an unfamiliar word can help you figure out the word's meaning. The antonym may appear in the same sentence as the unfamiliar word or in a separate sentence.

Example: After hearing the <u>din</u> of machines all day, workers were happy to leave the factory for the quiet of home.

Context clues: *Din* and *quiet* are antonyms.

Example: As a young man, Daniel always has a neat appearance. We can hardly remember how <u>unkempt</u> he used to look as a boy.

Context clues: *Unkempt* and *neat* are antonyms.

Exercises

Circle the antonym that can help you figure out the meaning of the underlined word.

1. Although she was <u>timid</u> as a child, today my sister is a fearless young woman.

2. Carlton insisted that his plan was <u>feasible</u>, but everyone else said it was impossible.

3. Alyson's anger did not <u>abate</u> over time. Instead, it increased.

 WRITING SKILL BUILDER

Writing a Paragraph

A well-written paragraph develops one main idea. You can state this idea in a topic sentence.

Activity

Country living is better than city living, because cities are crowded, noisy, and dangerous. Do you agree or disagree? Why?

Write a paragraph expressing your point of view. Begin by writing a topic sentence. Then write three sentences in which you support your position with specific reasons, facts, or examples. In your paragraph, use at least two of the words that you have learned in this lesson. Write your paragraph on a separate sheet of paper.

LESSON 4

Lesson Preview

Some of the words that you will encounter on pages 30–31 and 33–34 of this lesson appear in bold type in the following paragraph.

> Diana and Liz were as different as two sisters could be. Diana was **garrulous**. Liz usually remained silent. Diana was a wonderful cook who prepared **delectable** meals. Liz's meals were dreadful. On the other hand, Diana had an **insolent** nature, while Liz was respectful toward everyone.

In Lesson 3's *Vocabulary Skill Builder*, you learned how an antonym that appears before or after an unfamiliar word can help you figure out the word's meaning. Identify an antonym in the paragraph for each of the words in bold type.

 LESSON WORDS 1–10: Pronounce the word, spell it, study its meanings, and finish the sentence that follows it.

---

civil (*adj.*)   adequately polite; **mannerly**; **genteel**; **courteous**
ˈsi-vəl

  1. Avoid (foul, polite) _____ language; try to be more *civil.*

condense (*v.*)   reduce the extent of; express in fewer words;
kən-ˈden(t)s   **compress**; **abridge**

  2. The *condensed* edition is (twice, half) _____ the size of the original.

culpable (*adj.*)   deserving censure; **blameworthy**; **guilty**;
ˈkəl-pə-bəl   **reprehensible**

  3. If they are *culpable,* let us (condemn, praise) _____ them.

delectable (*adj.*)   very pleasing; **delightful**; **delicious**; **luscious**
di-'lek-tə-bəl

4. Some (like, dislike) _____ bananas, but others find them *delectable.*

edible (*adj.*)   fit for eating; **eatable**; **comestible**
'e-də-bəl

5. The only *edible* part of a walnut is the (shell, kernel) _____.

garrulous (*adj.*)   inclined to chatter to excess, especially about
'gar-ə-ləs   unimportant matters; **talkative**; **loquacious**

6. If you are *garrulous,* you will (bore, delight) _____ your audience.

gist (*n.*)   main point of a matter; **essence**; **core**; **pith**
'jist

7. The *gist* of a news story is in its (headline, ending) _____.

insolent (*adj.*)   boldly disrespectful; **insulting**; **impertinent**;
'in-sə-lənt   **impudent**; **rude**

8. Show (regard, contempt) _____ for the court; don't be *insolent.*

irk (*v.*)   **annoy**; **irritate**; **disgust**; **exasperate**; **vex**
'ərk

9. It *irks* voters when legislators (observe, violate) _____ the law.

knack (*n.*)   special skill for doing something; **gift**; **talent**; **flair**
'nak

10. Troubleshooters have a *knack* for (solving, creating) _____ problems.

SENTENCE COMPLETION 1–10: Enter the required lesson words.

1. Sheila is by nature _____; whenever she tells a story, her friends plead with her to _____ it.

2. Wouldn't it _____ you if your entire class were punished for something that only one or two classmates were _____ of?

3. I didn't particularly enjoy the meal; the food was _____ but not _____.

4. A good thinker has the _____ of getting quickly to the _____ of a problem, without wasting time on lesser matters.

5. Umpires usually have enough self-control to be _____ to a player who questions their judgment, even when that player is a bit _____.

VOCABULARY IN CONTEXT 1–10: Read the paragraph, and on a separate sheet of paper, answer the questions that follow. Do not repeat any of the underlined words in your answers; use synonyms instead.

My cousin Freddy never knows when to stop talking. He is a garrulous guy who simply cannot condense a story or just give you the gist of an event. Instead, he chatters on and on, describing every last detail. It's hard to be civil to Freddy. He's not a bad person, but his babbling really irks me.

1. How does the narrator feel toward Freddy? Why?

2. If Freddy was your cousin, how would you handle the situation?

LESSON WORDS 11–20: Pronounce the word, spell it, study its meanings, and finish the sentence that follows it.

---

literate (*adj.*)   able to read and write; **educated**; **cultured**
ˈli-tə-rət

    11.   (Nobody, Everyone) _____ has to be *literate* to watch TV.

mock (*v.*)   treat with scorn or contempt; **ridicule**; **taunt**; **deride**
ˈmäk

    12.   Even my friends might *mock* me if I misspelled (sinewy, cat) _____ .

obliging (*adj.*)   ready to do favors; **good-natured**; **amiable**;
ə-ˈblī-jiŋ   **accommodating**

    13.   *Obliging* classmates (sharpen, use) _____ my pencils.

prevail (*v.*)   be victorious; become dominant; **triumph**;
pri-ˈvā(ə)l   **predominate**

    14.   Unfortunately, (reason, ignorance) _____ sometimes *prevails*.

quell (*v.*)   put an end to; **suppress**; **crush**; **extinguish**
ˈkwel

    15.   All is quiet; the (disturbance, peace) _____ has been *quelled*.

queue (*n.*)   line of people or vehicles waiting their turn; **file**; **line**
ˈkyü

    16.   Shoppers on long *queues* tend to complain of the (prices, delay) _____ .

relish (*v.*)   take pleasure in; like the taste of; **savor**; **enjoy**; **like**
ˈre-lish

    17.   A (compliment, scolding) _____ is something we do not *relish*.

resolution (*n.*)   firmness of purpose; **determination**; **resolve**
,re-zə-'lü-shən

    18. His *resolution* to resist made it (hard, easy) _____
        for us to prevail.

verge (*n.*)   point beyond which something happens; **edge**; **brink**;
'vərj   **threshold**

    19. The (overfed, neglected) _____ pets were on the
        verge of starvation.

whim (*n.*)   sudden odd idea or desire; passing notion; **fancy**;
'hwim   **caprice**

    20. It is (risky, prudent) _____ to change course on the
        basis of a *whim*.

SENTENCE COMPLETION 11–20: Enter the required
lesson words from D, above.

---

  1. Ahead 6–0, the home team began to _____ us, but that
    only strengthened our _____ to win the game.

  2. The emperor was on the _____ of _____**ing**
    the uprising when his generals decided to join forces with the
    rebels.

  3. In our country, the rule of law _____**s**, rather than the
    _____ of some dictator.

  4. We do not _____ getting on the end of a slow-moving
    _____ when there is only one checkout counter.

  5. The youngsters will enjoy the book, even though they are not
    yet _____, if they can get _____ adults to read
    them a story from it.

VOCABULARY IN CONTEXT 11–20: Read the paragraph, and on a separate sheet of paper, answer the questions that follow. Do not repeat any of the underlined words in your answers; use synonyms instead.

It's a sad fact that not everyone in the world is <u>literate</u>. Through no fault of their own, some people have never even learned to write their name. As a result, others may <u>mock</u> them. This is cruel and unfair. Rather than make fun of someone's limitation, why not help the person overcome it? With <u>resolution</u> and hard work, the educated people of the world can <u>improve</u> the lives of those who are less fortunate. Knowledge can <u>prevail</u> over ignorance.

1. What is the main idea of this paragraph?

2. Do you think that the world's educated people have a responsibility to help those who are not literate? Why or why not?

SYNONYMS: To avoid repetition, replace the boldfaced word with a synonym from the vocabulary list below.

loquacious	savor	genteel	flair	exasperate
impertinent	reprehensible	deride	resolve	comestible

1. She **ridiculed** me; she said everything I did was ridiculous.

1. ＿＿＿＿＿＿＿**d**

2. Don't blame us; we are not **blameworthy**.

2. ＿＿＿＿＿＿＿＿

3. It **irritates** us to listen to irritating complaints.

3. ＿＿＿＿＿＿＿**s**

4. My brother is **courteous** to others, but he shows me no courtesy.

4. ＿＿＿＿＿＿＿＿

5. Lori is determined; we cannot say she lacks **determination**.

5. ＿＿＿＿＿＿＿＿

6. I didn't **like** the soup, but I liked the crispy breadsticks.

6. ＿＿＿＿＿＿＿＿

7. She has a **talent** for acting, but I am
   not a talented performer.   7. _____

8. He is very **talkative**; he keeps
   talking and talking.   8. _____

9. When campers are hungry, they eat
   anything that is **eatable**.   9. _____

10. Joe is not **disrespectful**; he respects
    everyone.   10. _____

 ANTONYMS: Enter the word most nearly the antonym of
the boldfaced word or words. Choose your antonyms from
the following list.

---

suppress	core	garrulous	comestible	abridge
illiterate	vex	predominate	courteous	blameworthy

1. Skip the **unimportant details**; let's discuss the _____
   of the problem.

2. You may very well be **guiltless**, but the others are clearly
   _____.

3. One cannot predict with certainty who will **lose** and who will
   _____.

4. A(n) _____ person with a secret cannot remain **close-
   mouthed** about it.

5. Chokecherries look _____, but they are **not fit to eat**.

6. That constant din apparently **did not irk** others, but it
   _____ed us.

7. His remarks are seldom _____; he has an **uncivil**
   tongue.

8. If we were _____, **educated** persons would have to
   read and write for us.

9. The rebellion was _____**ed**, and those who had
   fomented it fled.

10. I meant to **expand** my talk but had to _____ it for lack
    of time.

 CONCISE WRITING: Express the thought of each sentence
in NO MORE THAN FOUR WORDS.

---

1. The line of people who are waiting their turn keeps growing.

   _____

2. He is the sort of fellow who never does anyone a favor.

   _____

3. Grandma serves meals that are very pleasing to the taste.

   _____

4. The person who lives next door is inclined to talk too much
   about unimportant things.

   _____

5. Please express the motion that you are making in fewer words.

   _____

6. People who frequently go to the opera take pleasure in listening
   to the music that Puccini composed.

   _____

VOCABULARY SKILL BUILDER

Context Clues: Using Your Own Knowledge

You can often figure out an unfamiliar word by combining context clues with your own knowledge and experience.

> *Example:* For a long moment, the dog just stared at the food. Finally, he sniffed it, gave a little whine, and then backed away without tasting it. Even though he was hungry, he did not think the contents of the bowl were <u>edible</u>.

> *Context clues:* Would you eat something that looked and smelled bad? Based on your own knowledge and experience, you can conclude from the dog's behavior that he does not consider the food *edible*, or fit for eating.

Exercises

On a separate sheet of paper, explain how your knowledge and experience can help you figure out the meaning of each underlined word.

1. Kim <u>relished</u> the thought of summer vacation! She imagined herself lying on a beach, sipping cold drinks while listening to her favorite music.

2. When we saw the long <u>queue</u> outside the movie theater, we feared that the tickets would sell out before we could buy ours.

3. The teacher refused to put up with any more <u>insolent</u> behavior from the child. Maybe a trip to the principal's office would give the boy some time to think about the proper way to speak to a teacher.

WRITING SKILL BUILDER

Organization: Order of Increasing Importance

You develop an idea with supporting information. This information may include specific reasons, facts, or examples.

You can organize your supporting information in various ways. One method of organization is order of increasing importance. You arrange your reasons, facts, and examples in order from the least important or interesting to the most important or interesting. This method works especially well when you want to build up to a conclusion.

Activity

Should all junk food be banned from school vending machines and cafeterias? Write a paragraph expressing your views on this issue.

Begin by writing a topic sentence. Then write three sentences in which you support your position with specific reasons, facts, or examples. Organize your supporting information in order of increasing importance. In your paragraph, use at least two of the words that you have learned in this lesson. Write your paragraph on a separate sheet of paper.

Unit I Review and Enrichment

 CLOSE READING: Read the following statements. Then answer questions 1–10.

STATEMENTS

Eliza's dog Marbles was amazingly obedient; the first time I saw him, I said, "Roll over," and he did.

In selecting a crew for the *Hispaniola,* Squire Trelawney relied heavily on the advice of Long John Silver, a person he hardly knew.

Pocahontas begged her father, Powhatan, to spare John Smith's life.

After his expulsion from the Massachusetts Bay Colony, Roger Williams founded the colony of Rhode Island.

With rain threatening, the hostess of the picnic called for an immediate end to the volleyball game because the food was ready to be served.

No sooner did Walter give $6,500 to his partner Willie to invest in a liquor store, than Willie disappeared with the money.

Seeing a turtle in the road, Elsa guided it to a safe place in the tall grass.

Shelton's father said again and again, "I wish I had gone to college."

Francis Scott Key, who was on the scene when Fort McHenry was bombarded by a British fleet in 1814, wrote "The Star-Spangled Banner" the very next day.

Pamela bought her house for a very low price because so many other houses in her community were also for sale at the time.

QUESTIONS

1. Who was humane to an animal?_____

2. Who was defrauded?_____

3. Who rued something? _____

4. Who benefited from a glut? _____

5. Who condensed something? _____

6. Who lacked prudence? _____

7. Who was entreated? _____

8. Who was tractable? _____

9. Who was banned? _____

10. Who was subjected to a din? _____

CONCISE WRITING: Make the following composition more concise. The first paragraph has been rewritten as a sample. Rewrite the other paragraphs, trying to use no more than the number of words suggested.

Some Advice to Employees Who Have Just Joined the Company

Have confidence in those who are supervising your work, as well as in those of the same standing and ability as yourself. They are full of sympathy and consideration for others. If you consult them when you are in need of assistance with something or other, you will find them ready to do a favor for you. (*Cut to about 25 words, as in the lines below.*)

Have confidence in your supervisors and peers. They are humane. If you consult them when you need help, you will find them obliging.

If a door is closed, knock on that door before you walk in. At no time should you thrust yourself in without receiving a prior invitation to enter. (*Cut to about 10 words.*)

If you get a job to do that is capable of being done but difficult to do, do not throw up your hands in surrender. Go on with it, in spite of the difficulty. (*Cut to about 11 words.*)

_____

_____

If the person who has employed you ever expresses mild disapproval of you for paying little or no attention to your work, do not take offense but try to do better. (*Cut to about 17 words.*)

_____

_____

At all times, be open and honest in what you say or do. (*Cut to 3 words.*)

_____

 CLOSE READING: Read the following statements. Then answer questions 11–20.

STATEMENTS

Mom's message read: "We're safe. Tell you the rest later."

The Boston Tea Party was planned by Samuel Adams with the intention of provoking a war between England and the thirteen colonies.

Finding a beautiful, huge, wooden horse outside their walls, the Trojans hauled it into their city. That night, armed Greek warriors emerged from the horse and set fire to Troy.

When John Alden delivered Miles Standish's proposal of marriage to Priscilla, she said, "Why don't you speak for yourself, John?"

When True Son ran away, Cuyloga, his adoptive father, tracked him to his hiding place in the hollow of a tree.

Hearing that a band of Native Americans was approaching his settlement, Tonseten hid under his bed.

The Pied Piper played so enchantingly that all the children of Hamelin followed him.

In the middle of the night of April 18, 1775, John Hancock was warned by Paul Revere that British troops were coming to arrest him.

When Secretary of State Seward concluded the purchase of Alaska from Russia in 1867, many Americans called it "Seward's Folly."

Despite military setbacks and shortages of troops and supplies, George Washington refused to give up the fight for independence.

QUESTIONS

11. Who was timid? _____

12. Who led a horde? _____

13. Who was roused? _____

14. Who concocted a conflict?_____

15. Who persisted?_____

16. Who was mocked? _____

17. Who spurned someone? _____

18. Who conveyed the gist of something? _____

19. Who were victims of a sham? _____

20. Who was proficient as a sleuth? _____

ANALOGIES: Which lettered pair of words—a, b, c, d, or e—most nearly has the same relationship as the numbered pair? Enter the letter of your answer in the space provided. The first analogy question has been answered and explained as a sample.

1. BOGUS : GENUINE

    a. spacious : roomy   *b.* grateful : thankful
    c. careful : cautious   *d.* defective : perfect
    e. precious : valuable   1. ___*d*___

    Explanation: BOGUS and GENUINE are antonyms. The only lettered pair that consists of antonyms is **defective** and **perfect**.

2. ENEMY : INIMICAL

    a. prisoner : free   *b.* chatterbox : quiet
    c. artisan : clumsy   *d.* tyro : inexperienced
    e. ally : hostile   2. _____

3. ALTRUISTIC : SHARE

    a. embittered : forgive   *b.* recalcitrant : obey
    c. disobliging : cooperate   *d.* undecided : act
    e. grateful : appreciate   3. _____

4. CREST : WAVE

    a. mouth : river   *b.* dock : ship
    c. roof : building   *d.* rainbow : sky
    e. waste : haste   4. _____

5. FOMENT : QUELL

    a. abridge : expand   *b.* subside : abate
    c. interdict : prohibit   *d.* teem : swarm
    e. provoke : rouse   5. _____

E VOCABULARY SKILL BUILDER

On a separate sheet of paper, explain how you can use context clues and your own knowledge and experience to figure out the meaning of each underlined word.

1. When it comes to computers, Gina is an expert. There is nothing she can't make them do. I'm only a novice, having just bought my first computer.

2. To say that audience members were antagonistic toward the speaker is an understatement. They booed and hissed and stamped their feet. Some even started throwing crumpled-up paper balls.

3. A horde of fans surrounded the movie star. The mob of young people chanted her name and thrust papers at her in hopes of getting an autograph.

4. It irks me when friends arrive late for an appointment. I know that sometimes they can't help it, but it irritates me all the same.

LESSON 5

Some of the words that you will encounter on pages 46–47 and
49–50 of this lesson appear in bold type in the following paragraph.

> The **inclement** weather made us postpone our picnic. How-
> ever, it did not **deter** us from walking to the video store. The
> movie we rented turned out to be a **mediocre** adventure film
> about a group of people who go on a **trek** through the Sahara
> Desert. Because their journey seemed to drag on for about an
> **eon**, my interest in the film soon **waned**.

In Lesson 4's *Vocabulary Skill Builder*, you learned how you can
often figure out an unfamiliar word by combining context clues with
your own knowledge. How can your knowledge and experience help
you understand what this paragraph is about? Write your answer on
a separate sheet of paper.

 LESSON WORDS 1–10: Pronounce the word, spell it,
study its meanings, and finish the sentence that follows it.

---

abet (*v.*) encourage with aid or approval; **incite**; **instigate**;
ə-'bet **countenance**

  1. It is a (disservice, service) _____ to society to *abet*
     criminals.

astute (*adj.*) **shrewd**; **clever**; **sagacious**; **crafty**
ə-'st(y)üt

  2. One must not be (on, off) _____ guard with an
     astute opponent.

46

complex (*adj.*)   consisting of interconnected parts; difficult to
käm-'pleks   understand; **complicated**; **intricate**

> 3. A (tablespoon, calculator) _____ is a *complex*
> gadget.

conjecture (*n.*)   conclusion based on insufficient evidence;
kən-'jek-chər   **guesswork**; **supposition**

> 4. *Conjectures* (sometimes, never) _____ turn out to
> be right.

deter (*v.*)   restrain from acting; **discourage**; **dissuade**; **inhibit**
di-'tər

> 5. Winding roads *deter* (reckless, careful) _____ driv-
> ers from increasing their speed.

elude (*v.*)   slip away from; **escape**; **evade**; **avoid**
ē-'lüd

> 6. The convict *eluded* guards and remains (at large, behind
> bars) _____.

eon or **aeon** (*n.*)   extremely long and indefinite period of time;
'ē-ən *or* 'ē-,än   **age**; **eternity**

> 7. Our (planet, nation) _____ has been in existence
> for *eons*.

exonerate (*v.*)   free from blame or responsibility; **absolve**;
ig-'zä-nə-,rāt   **exculpate**; **vindicate**

> 8. Three were found (innocent, guilty) _____, and
> one was *exonerated*.

expedient (*adj.*)   suitable under the circumstances;
ik-'spē-dē-ənt   **advantageous**; **advisable**

> 9. In bad times, a company may find it *expedient* to (increase,
> reduce) _____ its workforce.

expire (*v.*)   come to an end; **cease**; **terminate**; **die**
ik-'spīr

> 10. Licenses *expiring* May 31 should be renewed (on, before)
> _____ June 1.

SENTENCE COMPLETION 1–10: Enter the required lesson words.

1. The earth's last dinosaurs _____**d** many _____**s** ago.

2. Inez thought it would not be _____ to bring up a(n) _____ issue when the members were tired and getting ready to adjourn.

3. Some fear the new policy may _____ drug users, rather than _____ them.

4. By _____ twists and turns, the fleet-footed quarterback _____**d** his pursuers.

5. If the charges rest solely on _____, the defendant should be _____**d**.

VOCABULARY IN CONTEXT 1–10: Read the paragraph, and on a separate sheet of paper, answer the questions that follow. Do not repeat any of the underlined words in your answers; use synonyms instead.

Even the most <u>astute</u> minds have no ready answers to the <u>complex</u> problems our planet faces. How can we feed all the hungry? Where will people live as the population grows? How can we protect the world's natural resources? The answers to such questions continue to <u>elude</u> scientists and politicians alike. However, nearly everyone agrees that cooperation among nations is necessary if we are to make any real progress.

1. What is the main idea of this paragraph?

2. Why are such problems as world hunger and population growth so complex?

LESSON WORDS 11–20: Pronounce the word, spell it, study its meanings, and finish the sentence that follows it.

inclement (*adj.*)   **stormy**; **rough**; **harsh**; **severe**
(,)in-'kle-mənt

    11. *Inclement* weather keeps most people (outdoors, indoors) _____ .

iota (*n.*)   very small quantity; infinitesimal amount; **bit**; **jot**; **mite**;
ī-'ō-tə   **smidgen**

    12. There is not an *iota* of doubt that the earth is (round, flat) _____ .

jibe (*v.*)   be in accord; **agree**; **correspond**; **conform**
'jīb

    13. Fans (boo, approve) _____ when an umpire's decision does not *jibe* with their expectations.

lethal (*adj.*)   causing or capable of causing death; **deadly**; **fatal**;
'lē-thəl   **mortal**

    14. We must be aware that carbon (monoxide, dioxide) _____ is a *lethal* gas.

maim (*v.*)   wound seriously; **cripple**; **mutilate**; **disfigure**
'mām

    15. The pirate with the wooden (club, leg) _____ had been *maimed* in battle.

mediocre (*adj.*)   neither good nor bad; barely adequate; **average**;
,mē-dē-'ō-kər   **inferior**

    16. Food prices (rise, fall) _____ whenever crops are *mediocre*.

obsolete (*adj.*)   no longer in use; **old-fashioned**; **outmoded**;
,äb-sə-'lēt   **out-of-date**

    17. Rail travel made the (stagecoach, automobile) _____ *obsolete*.

thrive (*v.*)   be fortunate; be successful; **prosper**; **flourish**
'thrīv

> 18. Those who (shun, seek) _____ work are not likely
> to *thrive*.

trek (*n.*)   **journey**; **expedition**; **trip**
'trek

> 19. (Planes, Books) _____ take us on *treks* to distant
> times and places.

wane (*v.*)   decrease in power, size, or extent; **abate**; **ebb**;
'wān   **subside**

> 20. As daylight *wanes,* the streetlights are gradually turned (on,
> off) _____ .

SENTENCE COMPLETION 11–20: Enter the required
lesson words from D, above.

---

1. Department-store sales were _____ this past week
   because of the _____ weather.

2. If fireworks are inexpertly used or are defective, they can
   _____ people, or even be _____ .

3. Your story _____**s** perfectly with his; there is not a(n)
   _____ of difference between them.

4. In today's fiercely competitive business world, manufacturers
   who use _____ equipment cannot possibly
   _____ .

5. We encountered so many difficulties in our last _____
   through the woods that my enthusiasm for hiking has
   _____**d**.

VOCABULARY IN CONTEXT 11–20: Read the paragraph, and on a separate sheet of paper, answer the questions that follow. Do not repeat any of the underlined words in your answers; use synonyms instead.

Besides the fact that fireworks are illegal in many places, they are also terribly dangerous. An error in judgment can <u>maim</u> someone for life. Even experienced adults have learned the hard way that fireworks can be <u>lethal</u>. Anyone with an <u>iota</u> of intelligence will leave fireworks to professionals.

1. What is the main idea of this paragraph?

2. Does this idea <u>jibe</u> with your views? Why or why not?

SYNONYMS: To avoid repetition, replace the boldfaced word with a synonym from the vocabulary list below.

complicated	evade	expedition	inferior	inhibit
instigate	outmoded	prosper	sagacious	terminate

1. We want excellence, not mediocrity; we will not be satisfied with **mediocre** results.

1. _____

2. Yours is a **complex** problem; mine is of much lesser complexity.

2. _____

3. That was a very **astute** move on your part; we are truly amazed by your remarkable astuteness.

3. _____

4. New equipment begins to obsolesce the day it is manufactured; in a few years it may well be **obsolete**.

4. _____

5. Bad weather is usually a deterrent, but it did not **deter** us from finishing our game.

5. _____

6. Our policy is about to **expire**; the
   expiration data is imminent.

   6. _____

7. The suspect is elusive; he has again
   eluded his pursuers.

   7. _____d

8. They trekked through unexplored
   forest; it was a perilous **trek**.

   8. _____

9. Your competitors do a thriving
   business. Why don't you **thrive**?

   9. _____

10. We certainly did not **abet** the
    protestors; someone else must have
    been the abettor.

    10. _____

 ANTONYMS: Enter the word most nearly the antonym of
the boldfaced word or words. Choose your antonyms from
the following list.

---

absolve	advisable	deadly	dissuade	supposition
expire	incite	intricate	smidgen	subside

1. What I thought was a **simple** problem turned out to be quite

   _____.

2. People and animals need food to **live**; without it, they would

   _____.

3. If the pain **increases**, I take my medicine and it begins to

   _____.

4. In crisis situations, actions normally **inexpedient** may be very
   definitely _____.

5. He **did not abet** the rioters; someone else _____d
   them.

6. The testimony may _____ the suspect rather than
   incriminate her.

7. There was not a **large amount** of leftovers—just a(n)

   _____.

8. Is this a **conclusion based on sufficient evidence**, or a(n) _____?

9. I didn't **encourage** her to resign; in fact, I tried to _____ her.

10. Smoking is decidedly not a **harmless** habit; it can be _____.

 CONCISE WRITING: Express the thought of each sentence in NO MORE THAN FOUR WORDS.

---

1. Rocks endure for extremely long and indefinite periods of time.

   _____

2. The grades that Lori has been getting are neither good nor bad.

   _____

3. Some accidents cause people to lose an arm, a leg, or the sight of an eye.

   _____

4. The conclusions that you have arrived at are in accord with mine.

   _____

5. Take whatever course of action is suitable under the circumstances.

   _____

6. The person who had been on trial was freed of all blame.

   _____

| J | **VOCABULARY SKILL BUILDER** |

Context Clues: Comparison

Writers often compare people, places, or things. Such comparisons can help you figure out what an unfamiliar word means.

Example: Following this recipe is as <u>complex</u> a task as assembling a 1,000-piece jigsaw puzzle.

Context clues: The writer compares following the recipe with doing a complicated puzzle. This comparison suggests the meaning of *complex*.

Example: Please handle this chemical with care. It's as <u>lethal</u> as rat poison.

Context clues: The writer compares the chemical with rat poison, suggesting the meaning of *lethal*.

Exercises

On a separate sheet of paper, explain how the comparison that the writer makes can help you figure out the meaning of each underlined word.

1. More and more people are writing on computers. Soon the typewriter will be as <u>obsolete</u> as the record player.

2. It was quite a <u>trek</u> to the bottom of the mountain, like hiking all the way down into the Grand Canyon.

3. Your <u>conjecture</u> about the outcome of the election is about as believable as my prediction of next week's weather.

WRITING SKILL BUILDER

Organization: Order of Decreasing Importance

You develop an idea with supporting information, such as reasons, facts, or examples. You can organize this information in various ways.

In Lesson 4's *Writing Skill Builder,* you learned one method of organization: order of increasing importance. Another method is order of *decreasing* importance. You arrange your reasons, facts, and examples in order from the most important or interesting to the least important or interesting. This method works well when you want to begin with a strong point and then follow with additional points.

Activity

Should people be allowed to own guns? This is an often debated question. What are your views on the issue? Write a paragraph expressing your point of view.

Begin by writing a topic sentence. Then write three sentences in which you support your position with specific reasons, facts, or examples. Organize your supporting information in order of decreasing importance. In your paragraph, use at least two of the words that you have learned in this lesson. Write your paragraph on a separate sheet of paper.

LESSON 6

Some of the words that you will encounter on pages 56–58 and 59–60 of this lesson appear in bold type in the following poem. Read the poem, and on a separate sheet of paper, answer the questions that follow.

> The **legendary** Bulls entered our gym.
> Their basketball talents were well-known.
> Our team was all but ready to **concede**
> When we saw how tall those players had grown.
>
> But the hometown crowd was behind us.
> Our spirit was **boosted** by their cheers.
> And as we trotted out onto the court,
> Self-confidence replaced our fears.
>
> Our fans **induced** us to try our best
> But, alas, some things hope cannot fix.
> Although we played the game of our lives,
> Those Bulls trampled us eighty to six.

What event does this poem describe? Is the poet a Bulls fan? How do you know?

LESSON WORDS 1–10: Pronounce the word, spell it, study its meanings, and finish the sentence that follows it.

---

adamant (*adj.*)   unyielding in attitude or opinion; **inflexible**;
'a-də-mənt   **uncompromising**

   1. Mediators may give (in, up) _____ if the opposing sides remain *adamant*.

boost (*v.*)   lift by pushing up from below; **raise**; **increase**;
'büst   **augment**

   2. The (jeers, cheers) _____ from the stands *boosted* our team's morale.

concede (*v.*)   admit grudgingly; **acknowledge**; **grant**
kən-'sēd

    3. The losers *conceded* that (we, they) _____ were
       the better team.

device (*n.*)   something devised or constructed for a particular
di-'vīs   purpose; **invention**; **contrivance**; **gadget**

    4. A (zipper, spool) _____ is a *device* for joining two
       pieces of cloth.

estimate (*v.*)   calculate approximately; **judge**; **figure**; **reckon**
'es-tə-,māt

    5. If you ask me to *estimate* a distance, I will tell you (roughly,
       exactly) _____ what I think it is.

extraction (*n.*)   **origin**; **birth**; **ancestry**; **descent**; **lineage**
ik-'strak-shən

    6. The ancestors of (most, all) _____ of us Americans,
       except Native Americans, were of foreign *extraction*.

foreboding (*n.*)   strong inner conviction of a coming misfortune;
(')fȯr-'bōd-iŋ   **apprehension**; **premonition**; **misgiving**

    7. We had a *foreboding* that *we* would (win, lose)

       _____ .

immaterial (*adj.*)   of no essential consequence; **unimportant**;
,i-mə-'tir-ē-əl   **irrelevant**

    8. The fact that I had forgotten my key was *immaterial* because
       my folks were home (before, after) _____ me.

impetus (*n.*)   driving force; **impulse**; **stimulus**
'im-pə-təs

    9. The possibility of a salary (freeze, increase) _____
       is an *impetus* to a greater effort.

induce (*v.*)   move someone to do something; **influence**;
in-'d(y)üs   **persuade**

    10. Logic cannot *induce* (reasonable, enraged) _____
        people to change their minds.

SENTENCE COMPLETION 1–10: Enter the required lesson
words.

1. Many Americans who are not of Irish _____ enjoy
   wearing green on St. Patrick's Day; the fact that they are not Irish
   is _____.

2. On March 15, 44 B.C., Julius Caesar's wife had a(n)
   _____ of evil and begged her husband to stay home,
   but she could not _____ him to obey her.

3. Even the most _____ foes of the proposed legislation
   _____ that they cannot stop it from becoming a law.

4. A jet engine is the _____ that produces an airliner's for-
   ward _____.

5. The corporation's president confidentially _____s that
   its new product could _____ earnings ten percent in
   the coming year.

VOCABULARY IN CONTEXT 1–10: Read the paragraph,
and on a separate sheet of paper, answer the questions
that follow. Do not repeat any of the underlined words in
your answers; use synonyms instead.

The remote control may be a useful <u>device</u>, but it is not a healthful one. It only encourages laziness. Thanks to the remote, television addicts never even have to get up. Nothing can <u>induce</u>
these viewers to move, except perhaps the need to use the bath-
room. Hunger may still be an <u>impetus</u> to leave the couch, but if
there is a telephone nearby, food can be delivered. No wonder
that health officials have a <u>foreboding</u> that overweight, out-of-
shape TV viewers will become increasingly common.

1. Why does the writer feel that the remote control is not a healthful device?

2. Do you agree with the writer's viewpoint? Why or why not?

LESSON WORDS 11–20: Pronounce the word, spell it, study its meanings, and finish the sentence that follows it.

---

legendary (*adj.*)   fabled in legend or tradition; **well-known**;
'le-jən-,der-ē   **famous**; **fabulous**

11. It is extremely (easy, hard) _____ to get tickets to the *legendary* violinist's rare concerts.

notorious (*adj.*)   widely but unfavorably known; **infamous**; **ill-**
nō-'tȯr-ē-əs   **famed**

12. (Many, Few) _____ were aware of the *notorious* dealer's reputation.

obstruct (*v.*)   block or close off by obstacles; **impede**; **hinder**;
äb-'strəkt   **bar**

13. A(n) (overturned, speeding) _____ vehicle was *obstructing* traffic.

opportune (*adj.*)   especially right or suitable; **timely**; **favorable**;
,ä-pər-'t(y)ün   **propitious**

14. Rain came at an *opportune* time; the reservoirs were (dry, full) _____ .

plummet (*v.*)   drop or fall sharply and abruptly; **plunge**;
'plə-mət   **nosedive**

15. A sudden (glut, dearth) _____ of tomatoes causes the price per pound to *plummet*.

repulse (*v.*)   drive back; beat back; **repel**; **check**
ri-'pəls

16. When our foes are *repulsed*, (they, we) _____ suffer a setback.

stamina (*n.*)   physical or moral strength to withstand hardship;
'sta-mə-nə   **endurance**; **perseverance**

    17. (Brawny, Frail) _____ people seem to lack *stamina* for heavy work.

subjugate (*v.*)   bring under complete control; **conquer**; **subdue**;
'səb-ji-ˌgāt   **crush**; **vanquish**

    18. A *subjugated* nation (loses, gains) _____ its independence.

unwavering (*adj.*)   not fluctuating or hesitant; **firm**; **sure**;
ˌən-'wāv-(ə-)riŋ   **steady**; **unfaltering**

    19. Their support is *unwavering*; they (usually, always) _____ back us.

venture (*n.*)   risky or dangerous undertaking; **adventure**;
'ven(t)-shər   **enterprise**

    20. Business *ventures* are not for people who are (loath, inclined) _____ to take chances.

SENTENCE COMPLETION 11–20: Enter the required lesson words from D, above.

---

1. The outnumbered defenders feared that their country would be ruthlessly _____**d** if they could not decisively _____ the invaders at the mountain pass.

2. Prices were _____**ing**; it was an exceptionally _____ time to buy.

3. The _____ criminal's only hope of avoiding conviction was to try to _____ justice by bribing one of the jurors.

4. We were stunned when the favorite, who is _____ for her _____, failed to complete the first lap in the 1,600-meter race.

5. In their _____ to win independence, the leaders of the
   American Revolution lacked the _____ support of the
   majority of Americans.

 VOCABULARY IN CONTEXT 11–20: Read the paragraph,
and on a separate sheet of paper, answer the questions
that follow. Do not repeat any of the underlined words in
your answers; use synonyms instead.

Many readers enjoy tales of medieval adventure. They love to
read about a <u>legendary</u> knight setting off on a thrilling <u>venture</u> to
do battle with a <u>notorious</u> foe. The brave warrior waits for an
<u>opportune</u> moment to strike. Then, with <u>unwavering</u> courage,
the hero leads an army to <u>repulse</u> the enemy.

1. According to the writer, what is a typical plot of a medieval
   adventure story?

2. Can a fictional character or a real-life person be both legendary
   and notorious? Explain your answer.

 SYNONYMS: To avoid repetition, replace the boldfaced
word or expression with a synonym from the vocabulary
list.

---

persuade	gadget	subdue	inflexible	reckon
fabulous	propitious	descent	infamous	impede

1. The athlete most responsible for the
   fame of the New York Yankees was Babe
   Ruth, their **famous** home-run hitter.   1. _____

2. Sue **estimated** that we would have
   a capacity crowd on opening night,
   and her estimate proved to be correct.   2. _____**ed**

3. A fallen tree trunk **obstructed** our
   advance, but we were able to climb
   over that obstruction.   3. _____**d**

4. The emperor Napoleon conquered most of Europe, but he could not **conquer** Russia.

4. _____

5. Our classmate Maria is of Hispanic **ancestry**; her ancestors lived in Puerto Rico.

5. _____

6. As a further inducement, the store lowered prices an additional 10%, but that **induced** only a few more customers to make purchases.

6. _____**d**

7. It is not yet fully known how the authorities were able to bring the **widely but unfavorably known** financier to justice.

7. _____

8. Your **uncompromising** attitude makes compromise impossible.

8. _____

9. The weather has turned inclement; it is certainly not a **timely** time for a stroll.

9. _____

10. Inventors have devised a variety of **devices** for simplifying household tasks.

10. _____**s**

 ANTONYMS: In the space provided in each sentence below, enter the word most nearly the antonym of the boldfaced word or expression. Choose your antonyms from the following list.

---

endurance	legendary	hinder	augment	acknowledge
irrelevant	subjugate	favorable	plunge	unfaltering

1. The hawk _____**d** earthward, seized its prey, and **soared**.

2. The American-led invasion of Europe in 1944 **liberated** nation after nation that the Nazis and their allies had _____**d**.

3. They _____**ed** your progress; we did **not bar** your way.

4. An increase in food prices is _____ when one is very wealthy, but **of vital consequence** when one is very poor.

5. They _____**d** that we outplayed them in the last two games, but they still **do not concede** that ours is the better team.

6. The sales staff was _____**ed** for the holiday shopping season and **reduced** as soon as it was over.

7. I expect my **weakness** to subside and my _____ to return.

8. It was an **inopportune** time for her to ask for a raise; she should have chosen a more _____ occasion.

9. By his achievements in the 1936 Olympics, Jesse Owens, a practically **unknown** athlete, became a(n) _____ hero.

10. Despite **wavering** support from some of the voters, the candidate was _____ in her determination to go on with her campaign.

 CONCISE WRITING: Express the thought of each sentence in NO MORE THAN FOUR WORDS.

---

1. Pizarro brought the people who were living in Peru under his complete control.

_____

2. Once in a while, everyone of us has strong inner convictions of approaching misfortune.

_____

3. Those who took part in the invasion were driven back.

_____

4. Did the risky undertaking that she entered into turn out to be a success?

_____

5. The questions that they asked were of no essential consequence.

_____

6. Some people do not have the physical or moral strength to withstand hardship.

_____

_____

| J | **VOCABULARY SKILL BUILDER** |

_____

Word Parts: Prefixes

Many words are made up of parts. For example, the word _inflexible_ has three parts:

_in-_	+	_flex_	+	_-ible_
prefix		root		suffix

Flex is a _root_, a word part from which other words are formed. _In-_ is a prefix, while _-ible_ is a suffix. _Prefixes_ and _suffixes_ are groups of letters added to the beginning (prefix) or end (suffix) of a word or root, changing its meaning or forming a new word.

Your knowledge of word parts can help you figure out the meaning of unfamiliar words and expand your vocabulary.

Some of the vocabulary words in this lesson use the common prefixes shown below:

Prefix	Meaning	Lesson Word
im-	"not"; "the opposite of"	immaterial
re-	"back"; "again"	repulse
sub-	"under"	subjugate
un-	"not"; "the opposite of"	unwavering

Exercises

Each of the following words appears as a synonym in this lesson. Circle the prefix in each word. Then write a brief definition. If you need help, check a dictionary.

1. unimportant   _____

2. subdue   _____

3. unfaltering   _____

4. repel   _____

5. impede   _____

6. uncompromising   _____

 WRITING SKILL BUILDER

Organization: Chronological (Time) Order

You have learned two ways to organize supporting information: order of increasing importance (page 39) and order of decreasing importance (page 55). Another method is chronological, or time, order.

Using this approach, you present facts, examples, or a series of events in sequence according to time: what happened first, what happened next, and so on. This method works well when you are describing how one event follows, or leads to, the next. Authors typically use chronological order to write historical accounts.

Activity

Choose a story or novel that you have recently read. Write a paragraph summarizing the plot. Describe the events in chronological order. In your paragraph, use at least two of the words that you have learned in this lesson. Write your paragraph on a separate sheet of paper.

LESSON 7

Some of the words that you will encounter on pages 66–67 and 69–70 of this lesson appear in bold type in the following paragraph.

> Being jealous of other people can only make you unhappy. What's to be gained by envying **affluent** people, wishing you had their riches? Rather than **covet** what others have, work to improve your own life. Don't let jealousy **thwart** your efforts. **Convert** any negative feelings to positive energy!

What is the main point of this paragraph? Do you agree with this point? Why or why not?

 LESSON WORDS 1–10: Pronounce the word, spell it, study its meanings, and finish the sentence that follows it.

---

affluent (*adj.*) having abundant goods or riches; **wealthy**;
ˈa-(ˌ)flü-ənt   **prosperous**; **opulent**

    1. You don't have to be *affluent* to own a (calculator, yacht)
    _____ .

aloof (*adj.*) distant in feeling or interest; **unconcerned**;
ə-ˈlüf   **indifferent**

    2. (Selfish, Humane) _____ people remain *aloof* when others suffer.

bolster (*v.*) prop up; **support**; **sustain**
ˈbōl-stər

    3. The (ominous, propitious) _____ news *bolstered* our spirits.

chore (*n.*)   small routine job around a house or farm; **task**;
'chór   **assignment**

    4. My *chore* this week is to (expand, vacuum) _____
the living room.

commitment (*n.*)   agreement to do something in the future;
kə-'mit-mənt   **pledge**; **promise**

    5. If you say you (may, will) _____ come, you are
making a *commitment*.

confederate (*n.*)   person allied with another or others;
kən-'fə-d(ə)-rət   **accomplice**; **ally**

    6. The bank robber was (arrested, aided) _____ by a
confederate.

convert (*v.*)   change in form from one state to another; **transform**;
kən-'vərt   **alter**

    7. (Falling, Rising) _____ temperatures *convert* slush
to ice.

covet (*v.*)   wish for enviously or excessively; **desire**; **crave**
'kə-vət

    8. (Jealous, Generous) _____ youngsters *covet* their
playmates' toys.

crestfallen (*adj.*)   with hanging head; **dejected**; **disheartened**;
'krest-,fó-lən   **downcast**

    9. The (vanquished, victorious) _____ contender was
crestfallen.

infer (*v.*)   reach a conclusion by reasoning from facts; **conclude**;
in-'fər   **deduce**

    10. If the lights are (out, on) _____, we may *infer* the
store is closed.

SENTENCE COMPLETION 1–10: Enter the required lesson words.

1. While Cinderella swept ashes from the hearth and did all the other unpleasant _____**s**, her smiling stepsisters stood _____.

2. By _____**ing** the spirits of the _____ players, the coach got them to rally and to win the game.

3. Though the actress's successful movies have made her _____, they have not won her what she _____**s** most—an Oscar.

4. Lady Macbeth, by goading her husband, _____**s** his loyalty to King Duncan into a(n) _____ to murder him.

5. The evidence led investigators to _____ that the prisoner could not have escaped without help from a(n) _____.

VOCABULARY IN CONTEXT 1–10: Read the paragraph, and on a separate sheet of paper, answer the questions that follow. Do not repeat any of the underlined words in your answers; use synonyms instead.

Tina tried to keep busy cleaning up and doing other <u>chores</u> around the house. Although she told herself not to think about the mail, she couldn't help but listen for the mail carrier's footsteps. She whistled cheerful tunes to <u>bolster</u> her spirits, but happy songs could not <u>convert</u> her nervousness to calm. Finally, the mail arrived. She tore open the envelope and read the letter. The words left her <u>crestfallen</u>.

1. What was Tina's mood before receiving the letter? How do you know?

2. What can you <u>infer</u> about the contents of the letter?

LESSON WORDS 11–20: Pronounce the word, spell it, study its meanings, and finish the sentence that follows it.

mar (*v.*)   detract from the perfectness of; **spoil**; **damage**; **impair**;
'mär   **tarnish**

   11. We won, but an (injury, award) _____ to a player *marred* our victory.

obliterate (*v.*)   remove all traces of; destroy utterly; **erase**; **efface**
ə-'bli-tə-ˌrāt

   12. Use a(n) (comma, eraser) _____ to *obliterate* what you have written.

rile (*v.*)   make angry or resentful; **irritate**; **provoke**; **peeve**
'rī(ə)l

   13. A close decision against our (team, foes) _____ *riles* us.

robust (*adj.*)   strong and healthy; **hardy**; **vigorous**
rō-'bəst

   14. After a(n) (vacation, illness) _____, one is unlikely to look *robust*.

site (*n.*)   place where something is or was; **location**; **point**; **spot**
'sīt

   15. We looked for Franklin's (birthplace, writings) _____, but we couldn't find the *site*.

steep (*adj.*)   sharply rising or falling; **abrupt**; **precipitous**; **sheer**
'stēp

   16. A vehicle gains speed as it goes (up, down) _____ a *steep* slope.

surface (*n.*)   outermost or uppermost layer or area; **top**; **exterior**;
'sər-fəs   **outside**

   17. At night, (all, half) _____ the earth's *surface* is cloaked in darkness.

thwart (*v.*)   prevent (someone) from achieving a purpose;
'thwȯrt   **frustrate; foil; baffle**

> 18. Loafers are *thwarted* when they cannot (find, avoid)
> _____ work.

turbulence (*n.*)   state of wild disorder; **commotion; agitation;**
'tər-byə-lən(t)s   **turmoil**

> 19. On a (calm, windy) _____ day, there is no *turbu-
> lence* in the atmosphere.

vestige (*n.*)   visible mark left by something vanished; **relic; trace**
'ves-tij

> 20. (Soaring, Plummeting) _____ temperatures
> removed all *vestiges* of yesterday's snow.

SENTENCE COMPLETION 11–20: Enter the required
lesson words from D, above.

---

1. If you were repeatedly _____**ed** in your attempts to
   talk to the manager by being put on hold, wouldn't you be
   _____**d**?

2. A couple of objects, probably snowballs, struck our windshield
   but did not _____ its _____.

3. The _____**er** the hill, the more _____ a jog-
   ger has to be to make it unwinded to the top.

4. Boats carefully avoid the waters close to the falls because of the
   river's _____ at that _____.

5. The devastating eruption of Vesuvius that occurred in A.D. 79
   _____**d** Pompeii from the face of the earth, leaving no
   _____ of that flourishing Italian town.

VOCABULARY IN CONTEXT 11–20: Read the paragraph, and on a separate sheet of paper, answer the questions that follow. Do not repeat any of the underlined words in your answers; use synonyms instead.

Captain Jim buried the pirates' treasure at a <u>site</u> deep in the woods. Then he took great pains to <u>obliterate</u> all signs that he had ever been there. He piled rocks and branches on the surrounding <u>surface</u>. He even wiped away all <u>vestiges</u> of his footprints. Then he used a secret code to write down the treasure's location.

Do you think that Captain Jim's efforts will thwart other people's attempts to find the treasure? Why or why not?

SYNONYMS: Replace the boldfaced word or expression with a synonym from the word list below.

indifferent	pledge	relic	sustain	tarnish
opulent	provoke	hardy	chore	dejected

1. Some are **disheartened** when they lose a game, but others do not take such matters to heart.

    1. _____

2. When I finish this task, I have other little **tasks** to do.

    2. _____**s**

3. As we retraced our steps, we saw **traces** that we had not noticed previously of an oil slick that had washed ashore.

    3. _____**s**

4. If you become **rich**, what will you do with your riches?

    4. _____

5. Our allies needed support; if we had not **supported** them, they might have collapsed.

    5. _____**ed**

6. A spoilsport may say or do things to **spoil** a happy occasion.

    6. _____

7. She was angry at me, though I had
   done nothing to **make** her **angry**.   7. _____

8. Some showed concern for the victim;
   others seemed **unconcerned**.   8. _____

9. Though the contestants all look
   vigorous, some may not have the
   vigor to finish the marathon.   9. _____

10. He promised to join, but he didn't
    keep his **promise**.   10. _____

 ANTONYMS: In the blank in each sentence below, enter
the word most nearly the antonym of the boldfaced word
or words. Choose your antonyms from the following list.

exterior	frustrate	transform	downcast	precipitous
spurn	prosperous	aloof	bolster	turmoil

1. Many who used to **crave** cigarettes now _____ them
   when offered.

2. All of us are **overjoyed** at the good news, but why are you
   _____?

3. Through hard work, Andrew Carnegie, a very **poor** immigrant,
   became one of the most _____ Americans of his time.

4. What goes on **inside** the earth is not usually visible on its
   _____.

5. While one group was trying to _____ the struggling
   new government, others were doing their best to **pull out the
   props from under** it.

6. We enjoy the **calm** that follows the _____ of a storm.

7. Sometimes circumstances **help** us achieve our purpose, and at
   other times they _____ us.

8. The entrance was completely _____**ed**; the rest of the
   house was **not altered**.

9. We cannot remain _____ when there is damage to the environment; we must be deeply **concerned**.

10. **Gradual** price increases are a nuisance, but _____ ones are altogether intolerable.

CONCISE WRITING: Express the thought of each sentence in NO MORE THAN FOUR WORDS.

---

1. People in foreign lands enviously wish for the freedoms that we enjoy.

   _____

2. No one made any agreements to do anything in the future.

   _____

3. What was the conclusion that you arrived at by the process of reasoning?

   _____

4. Showers detracted from the perfectness of the parade that we took part in.

   _____

5. Patricia finished the small routine jobs that she has to do.

   _____

6. The person that he is allied with is widely but unfavorably known.

   _____

VOCABULARY SKILL BUILDER

Context Clues: Contrast

In Lesson 5 (page 54), you learned how comparisons can help you figure out the meaning of an unfamiliar word. Sometimes writers *contrast*, or highlight differences between, people, places, or things.
Contrast is another context clue that can help you determine a word's
meaning.

> *Example:* The west side of Springville was the poor section of
> town, where homes were small, and every house
> seemed in need of repair. The east side, with its
> huge houses and perfectly green lawns, was clearly
> the more <u>affluent</u> part of the community.

> *Context clues:* The writer contrasts the two parts of Springville.
> This contrast suggests the meaning of *affluent*.

> *Example:* The thrilling soccer game ended with the jubilant
> winners screaming and jumping up and down while
> the <u>crestfallen</u> losers walked slowly off the field.

> *Context clues:* The writer contrasts the winners and losers, suggest-
> ing the meaning of *crestfallen*.

Exercises

On a separate sheet of paper, explain how contrast can help you figure out the meaning of each underlined word.

1. Aliya is a very different person inside than she appears to be on
   the <u>surface</u>.

2. Unlike the <u>steep</u> northern face of the mountain, the south side
   had a gradual slope.

3. Near the thunderous falls, the <u>turbulence</u> of the river made it
   impossible to cross. However, a mile below the falls, the water
   calmed down, and the current became almost gentle.

WRITING SKILL BUILDER

Developing Content: Comparison/Contrast

When you write, you may want to compare or contrast people, places, or things. When you compare, you describe similarities. When you contrast, you describe differences.

Sometimes you want to compare *and* contrast. For example, if you were writing about your experiences in school this year and last year, you might begin by talking about how the two years are alike. Then you might discuss ways in which they differ.

Activity

Do you think its easier or harder to be a child today than it was when your parents were young? Why? Write a paragraph expressing your views on this question.

Begin by writing a topic sentence. Then write at least three sentences in which you support your main idea with specific reasons, facts, or examples. Use comparison/contrast to develop your content. In your paragraph, use at least two of the words that you have learned in this lesson. Write your paragraph on a separate sheet of paper.

LESSON 8

Some of the words that you will encounter on pages 76–77 and
79–80 of this lesson appear in bold type in the following poem. Read
the poem, and on a separate sheet of paper, answer the questions
that follow.

> "The early bird gets the worm"
> Is an **adage** that's well-known,
> But let me **dispel** that whole idea,
> Because it always makes me groan.
>
> Let others get up early,
> If worms are what they choose.
> I prefer to **linger** in bed
> And get an extra snooze.

What opinion does the poet express? Do you agree with the poet?
Why or why not?

 LESSON WORDS 1–10: Pronounce the word, spell it,
study its meanings, and finish the sentence that follows it.

---

adage (*n.*)   old saying commonly accepted as a truth; **proverb**;
ˈa-dij   **byword**

   1. The *adage* "Haste makes waste" cautions us not to (delay,
     hurry) _____.

cajole (*v.*)   persuade by flattery or promises; **coax**; **wheedle**;
kə-ˈjōl   **sweet-talk**

   2. People who (like, hate) _____ to be overpraised
     cannot be *cajoled.*

chagrin (*n.*)   mental distress caused by failure or disappointment;
shə-'grin   **shame; mortification; humiliation**

   3. To their *chagrin*, the world champions finished (last, first)
     _____ .

clique (*n.*)   narrow, small, exclusive group of people; **circle;**
'klēk   **coterie; set**

   4. The members of a *clique* usually (welcome, reject)
     _____ outsiders.

derogatory (*adj.*)   expressing a low opinion; **belittling;**
di-'rä-gə-,tór-ē   **disparaging; slighting**

   5. It is *derogatory* to be called a (whiz, dolt) _____ .

dispel (*v.*)   drive away; **scatter; dissipate**
di-'spel

   6. The (setting, rising) _____ sun *dispelled* the fog.

fad (*n.*)   fashion or manner of conduct followed for a time; **style;**
'fad   **craze; rage**

   7. Conservatives tend to (reject, embrace) _____ a
     new *fad*.

illustrious (*adj.*)   highly distinguished; **eminent; famous;**
i-'ləs-trē-əs   **renowned**

   8. People are (eager, loath) _____ to see *illustrious*
     performers.

incarcerate (*v.*)   put in prison; **jail; confine**
in-'kär-sə-,rāt

   9. Convicts are *incarcerated* in the state (legislature, peniten-
     tiary) _____ .

indignation (*n.*)   righteous anger; strong displeasure; **ire; wrath**
,in-dig-'nā-shən

   10. (Victims, Scofflaws) _____ deserve the public's
     indignation.

SENTENCE COMPLETION 1–10: Enter the required lesson words.

1. Elsie's _____ was aroused when she heard that Bill, whom she had often helped with his homework, was making _____ remarks about her.

2. It was much to the _____ of the zookeeper that, with a large crowd looking on, he could not _____ the lioness back into her cage.

3. Janice felt that she would have to follow the latest _____ **s** in attire to be accepted into Marcy's _____.

4. Many _____ prisoners, like Sir Walter Raleigh and the Earl of Essex, were _____**d** in the infamous Tower of London.

5. Carl tried to _____ my sadness by reciting the _____, "It is always darkest just before the dawn."

VOCABULARY IN CONTEXT 1–10: Read the paragraph, and on a separate sheet of paper, answer the questions that follow. Do not repeat any of the underlined words in your answers; use synonyms instead.

Cliques of teenagers sometimes act cruelly toward outsiders. They may make derogatory remarks about their clothing or express indignation about their behavior. Teens who act unkindly toward others need to be reminded of the adage "treat others as you want others to treat you." As many soon learn, the day may come when the insiders become the outsiders.

1. What is the main idea of this paragraph?

2. Would you feel chagrin if you saw your best friend treat a new classmate unkindly? Explain your answer.

LESSON WORDS 11–20: Pronounce the word, spell it, study its meanings, and finish the sentence that follows it.

linger (*v.*)   be slow in leaving; **tarry**; **loiter**; **stay**
'liŋ-gər

11. I might have *lingered* if I had (nothing, chores) _____ to do.

numb (*adj.*)   deprived of the power to feel or move; **deadened**;
'nəm   **paralyzed**; **desensitized**

12. That day, I couldn't (budge, breathe) _____; I was *numb* with fear.

ostentatious (*adj.*)   intended to attract notice; **pretentious**;
,äs-tən-'tā-shəs   **showy**; **splashy**

13. Coming to school by (bus, limousine) _____ may be considered *ostentatious*.

plausible (*adj.*)   apparently worthy of belief; **credible**; **believable**
'plȯ-zə-bəl

14. There can be (no, some) _____ doubt about the truth of a *plausible* excuse.

probe (*n.*)   searching examination; **investigation**; **inquiry**
'prōb

15. A *probe* must not (ignore, investigate) _____ rumors.

prodigious (*adj.*)   of great size, power, or extent; **enormous**;
prə-'di-jəs   **huge**; **immense**

16. (Chickens, Oxen) _____ are legendary for their *prodigious* strength.

rankle (*v.*)   cause bitter resentment in; **irritate**; **embitter**;
'raŋ-kəl   **inflame**

17. When they (evade, keep) _____ their commitments, elected officials *rankle* the voters.

scant (*adj.*)   not quite enough; **meager**; **insufficient**
'skant

    18. The Devils led by a *scant* margin; the score was 31 to (30, 12) _____ .

surveillance (*n.*)   close watch; **supervision**; **scrutiny**
sər-'vā-lən(t)s

    19. *Surveillance* of the ruler's residence was (tightened, relaxed) _____ after several threats.

sustain (*v.*)   bear up under; **endure**; **undergo**; **suffer**
sə-'stān

    20. The physician considers the patient too (robust, frail) _____ to *sustain* surgery.

SENTENCE COMPLETION 11–20: Enter the required lesson words from D, above.

---

1. Throughout the yearlong _____ of the jewelry theft, the chief suspects were continuously under police _____ .

2. The evidence is too _____ to make a(n) _____ case against any of the suspects.

3. The losses that investors _____**ed** in the stock market crash of 1929 were _____ .

4. Marie Antoinette's _____ wardrobe and banquets _____**d** the French common people.

5. We couldn't _____ any longer at the picnic because our hands and feet were turning _____ from the cold.

F

VOCABULARY IN CONTEXT 11–20: Read the paragraph, and on a separate sheet of paper, answer the questions that follow. Do not repeat any of the underlined words in your answers; use synonyms instead.

Jason stood before the <u>ostentatious</u> home and shook his head. The sheer size of the house left him feeling <u>numb</u>. Could this really be Carlton's? Years ago, when they were in high school together, Carlton was not exactly known for <u>prodigious</u> brain power. In fact, he paid <u>scant</u> attention to his studies and never got higher than a *C*. He spent all his time on the basketball court, dreaming of becoming a professional player. Well, either his old friend's dream had come true, Jason thought, or else he had won the lottery. Neither explanation seemed <u>plausible</u>.

1. What is the main idea of this paragraph?

2. Suppose you were Jason. Would Carlton's apparent success <u>rankle</u> you? Why or why not?

G

SYNONYMS: To avoid repetition, replace the boldfaced word or expression with a synonym from the vocabulary below.

mortification	**coterie**	**inquiry**	**endure**	**ire**
scrutiny	**eminent**	**wheedle**	**proverb**	**pretentious**

1. At the time they were under **close watch**, they had no idea that they were being watched.

   1. _____

2. Why are you indignant? What did I do to arouse your **indignation**?

   2. _____

3. One of my neighbors tries to impress others by wearing flashy clothes, but the others are not **flashy** dressers.

   3. _____

4. Though they have **suffered** many financial losses, their style of living does not seem to have suffered.

   4. _____ **d**

5. An old **saying** says, "Empty barrels make loud noises."

5. _____

6. Imagine my **humiliation**! Never had I felt so humiliated!

6. _____

7. Don't try to **sweet-talk** us; we don't respond to sweet talk.

7. _____

8. I object to your **small exclusive group** because it excludes outsiders.

8. _____

9. Our **highly distinguished** guest of honor has distinguished herself in many ways.

9. _____

10. A team of skilled investigators is conducting the **investigation**.

10. _____

ANTONYMS: In the space provided in each sentence below, enter the word most nearly the antonym of the boldfaced word or words. Choose your antonyms from the following list.

---

credible	loiter	meager	**slighting**	showy
immense	intern	renowned	desensitized	wrath

1. **Little** acorns can grow into _____ oaks.

2. There was **ample** rain upstate, but here the precipitation was _____.

3. **Be quick in leaving**; don't _____.

4. One of the sisters is a(n) _____ attorney; the other has had an **undistinguished** career.

5. Only two of the witnesses seemed _____; the rest were **unworthy of belief**.

6. You have made many _____ remarks about the candidates, but you haven't said one **complimentary** word about any of them.

7. When your dentist injects novocaine, the immediate area becomes _____, but the rest of the mouth is **not deprived of feeling**.

8. The rebels **liberated** all the political prisoners that the ousted dictator had _____**ed**.

9. My _____ was aroused when I was overcharged, but after the manager apologized for the error, I had a feeling of **gratification**.

10. The building now has a(n) _____ exterior, but on the inside it is still **unostentatious**.

CONCISE WRITING: Express the thought of each sentence in NO MORE THAN FOUR WORDS.

---

1. Those who have been found guilty of criminal offenses should be put behind prison bars.

   _____

2. Was the searching investigation that was conducted worth all the time, money, and effort that was put into it?

   _____

3. Did the alibi that she offered appear to be worthy of belief?

   _____

4. That narrow, small, exclusive group of people meets every day of the week.

   _____

5. Critics who write reviews are often the cause of bitter resentment in authors who are in the profession of writing plays.

   _____

6. Every one of us has experienced the mental distress that comes on the heels of failure or disappointment.

   _____

| J | **VOCABULARY SKILL BUILDER** |

Word Parts: Suffixes

In Lesson 6 (page 64), you learned that many words are made up of parts, such as prefixes and suffixes. Recognizing word parts can help you figure out the meaning of words.

A suffix is a group of letters added to the end of a word or root, changing its meaning or forming a new word. Some of the vocabulary words and synonyms that you have seen in Lessons 1–8 use the common suffixes shown below:

Suffix	Meaning	Word
-able	capable of being; worthy of being	advisable, ungovernable, doable
-ion, -tion, -sion	action, state, or condition	resolution, invention, agitation
-ing	used to form an adjective	obliging, threatening, insulting

Exercises

1. Each of the following words appears as a synonym in this lesson. Circle the suffix in each word. Then write a brief definition. If you need help, check a dictionary.

   a. believable _____

   b. investigation _____

   c. humiliation _____

   d. disparaging _____

   e. supervision _____

2. Many words have both a prefix and a suffix. For example, the word *unwavering* appeared in Lesson 6.

   a. Identify the suffix *and* the prefix in *unwavering* (see the prefixes listed on page 64). Then use the word in a sentence. If you need help, check a dictionary.

   _____

   _____

   b. How did recognizing the prefix and suffix help you to understand the word's meaning and use?

   _____

   _____

 WRITING SKILL BUILDER

Writing a Paragraph

You have learned various ways to organize and develop content: order of increasing importance (page 39), order of decreasing importance (page 55), chronological order (page 65), and comparison/contrast (page 75).

Activity

Which of the following statements do you agree with?

- Males have easier lives than females.
- Females have easier lives than males.

Write a paragraph expressing your views. Start by writing a topic sentence. Then support and develop your main idea with specific reasons, facts, or examples. In your paragraph, use at least two of the words that you have learned in this lesson. Write your paragraph on a separate sheet of paper.

Unit II Review and Enrichment

CLOSE READING: Read the following statements. Then answer questions 1–10.

STATEMENTS

Anyone foolish enough to make a comment about the size of Cyrano de Bergerac's nose was almost certain to be challenged by him to a duel.

The night before the Battle of Philippi, Brutus had a strong inner feeling that he would not survive.

The brontosaurus, one of the dinosaurs that formerly dominated the earth, was about sixty feet long and weighed about twenty tons.

Though told that it was madness to seek revenge on Moby Dick, the white whale that had maimed him, Captain Ahab remained determined to pursue the monster.

People regarded Benedict Arnold as a brave and talented military leader, but they changed their opinion of him when he betrayed his country to the enemy.

The alchemists have been thwarted since the Middle Ages in their search for a way to turn base metals into gold.

Everything was going well at a party of the gods and goddesses on Mount Olympus until Eris, the Goddess of Discord, arrived uninvited.

The thirteen colonies rebelled against England because they wanted to be free.

When Claggart falsely accused Billy Budd of plotting a mutiny, Billy hit him once, killing him instantly.

The French fleet played a key role in Washington's defeat of the British army at Yorktown in 1781.

QUESTIONS

1. Who thrived aeons ago? _____

2. Who was dealt a lethal blow? _____

3. Whose reputation plummeted? _____

4. Who was bolstered? _____

5. Who had a foreboding? _____

6. Who wanted to convert something? _____

7. Who was sensitive to derogatory remarks? _____

8. Who refused to be subjugated? _____

9. Who adamantly adhered to a purpose? _____

10. Who marred a festive occasion? _____

B **CONCISE WRITING:** Make the following composition more concise. The first paragraph has been rewritten as a model. Rewrite the other paragraphs, trying to use no more than the number of words suggested.

Romeo Meets Juliet

The Montagues and the Capulets were two families with an abundance of wealth who lived in the city of Verona, and who had nothing but bitter hatred for each other. Every now and then, when they met on the streets of the city, there was a chance that swords might be drawn, and one or more members of the Montague family, or of the Capulet family, or of both families, might lose an arm, a leg, or the sight of an eye, or even be killed in a bloody fight. (*Cut to about 35 words.*)

The Montagues and Capulets, two affluent families of Verona, were bitter enemies. Occasionally, when they met on the streets, swords might be drawn, and one or more of them might be maimed or killed.

Romeo, who is a young man still in his teens, and the son of Lord Montague, believes himself to be in love with Rosaline. However, she remains distant in feeling and interest, and does not return his love. Learning that Rosaline has been invited to attend a masquerade party being given that very night by the Capulet family, Romeo is determined to go there, in the hope that he might see her. (*Cut to about 35 words.*)

That evening, as Romeo and his friend Mercutio, who are wearing masks, enter the palace of the Capulets, Romeo has a strong inner conviction of a coming misfortune. The instant he sees Juliet, Lord Capulet's beautiful daughter, who is not yet fourteen years of age, and she sees him, the two of them fall in love at first sight. However, Romeo is recognized by Juliet's cousin Tybalt, who has a temper that cannot be controlled. (*Cut to about 50 words.*)

The presence of Romeo causes bitter resentment in Tybalt; he calls for a servant to bring him his sword at once, so that he might kill the intruder. Fortunately, he is prevented from achieving this purpose by Lord Capulet, who does not want anything to happen that might detract from the perfection of the evening. (*Cut to about 30 words.*)

_____

_____

_____

_____

_____

_____

_____

 CLOSE READING: Read the following statements. Then answer questions 11–20.

STATEMENTS

"Fish and visitors smell in three days" is one of the many old sayings that Benjamin Franklin quoted in his *Poor Richard's Almanac*.

President Theodore Roosevelt, too weak as a child to attend school, became world famous as an adult for his physical endurance.

The entrance to the underworld in Greek mythology was closely guarded by Cerberus, a three-headed dog.

In the 1970s, Oscars and a Pulitzer Prize in Music were awarded to Scott Joplin, composer of "Maple Leaf Rag," who had died in 1917 at the age of 49.

Without thinking of all the possible consequences, King Midas wished that everything he touched might turn to gold.

For his defiance of the Greek gods, Atlas was condemned forever to bear the world on his shoulders.

The voyage around the world that Ferdinand Magellan led in 1519 showed once and for all that the world is not flat.

When Lewis and Clark explored the Pacific Northwest in 1804–05, Sacagawea—accompanied by her baby—joined them as a guide and interpreter.

After serving as vice president from 1801 to 1805, Aaron Burr was three times tried for treason and three times acquitted.

By drugging the drinks of King Duncan's bodyguards, Lady Macbeth made it easier for Macbeth to murder the king.

QUESTIONS

11. Who sustained a prodigious burden? _____

12. Who was exculpated? _____

13. Who abetted a criminal?_____

14. Who used adages? _____

15. Who acquired legendary stamina?_____

16. Who apparently had scant recognition while alive? _____

17. Who was a consultant on a trek? _____

18. Who helped dispel an erroneous belief? _____

19. Who coveted wealth? _____

20. Who maintained surveillance? _____

ANALOGIES: Which lettered pair of words—a, b, c, d, or e—most nearly has the same relationship as the numbered pair? Enter the letter of your answer in the space provided.

1. OBSOLETE : CURRENT
   - *a.* loath : willing
   - *b.* abundant : plentiful
   - *c.* adept : proficient
   - *d.* humane : altruistic
   - *e.* uncivil : insolent

   1. _____

2. IMPETUS : MOVE

    a. fog : see   *b.* lullaby : sleep

    c. din : relax   *d.* gag : speak

    e. illness : work   2. _____

3. INVINCIBLE : SUBJUGATE

    a. truthful : believe   *b.* corruptible : bribe

    c. adamant : persuade   *d.* flexible : influence

    e. employable : hire   3. _____

4. OPULENT : INCOME

    a. mediocre : talent   *b.* reckless : caution

    c. popular : following   *d.* astute : trap

    e. clumsy : skill   4. _____

5. IRRITABLE : RILE

    a. unruly : control   *b.* adamant : persuade

    c. determined : thwart   *d.* prudent : outwit

    e. unwary : bilk   5. _____

E   VOCABULARY SKILL BUILDER

---

1. On a separate sheet of paper, explain how you can use context clues and your own knowledge and experience to figure out the meaning of each underlined word.

    a. The forecast called for <u>inclement</u> weather, but the day turned out to be clear and sunny.

    b. Beth heard the plate crash to the floor and saw the cat come running out of the kitchen. Like a detective at a crime scene, she could <u>infer</u> what had happened.

    c. At first, David's older sister encouraged him to ride the roller coaster. However, when she saw just how fast it moved, she tried to <u>deter</u> him.

2. On a separate sheet of paper, explain the difference between a prefix and a suffix. Then give two examples of words you have studied that have these parts.

Cumulative Review
for Units I and II

A Circle the word that best completes each sentence.

1. The lawyer found new evidence to _____ the accused man of all charges against him.

     a. abate   b. chide   c. exonerate   d. elude

2. "Your fears are _____," Martha insisted. "Ghosts do not exist."

     a. groundless   b. expedient   c. adamant   d. derogatory

3. The child's constant whining was starting to _____ his mother.

     a. condense   b. irk   c. obstruct   d. covet

4. I want to hear the truth, so please be as _____ as you can.

     a. counterfeit   b. illustrious   c. candid   d. affluent

5. After years of household repair work, Chris had become _____ with tools.

     a. antagonistic   b. proficient   c. unkempt   d. robust

6. Thanks to her spies, the queen learned of the plot and managed to _____ the duke's plan to attack the castle.

     a. thwart   b. convert   c. bolster   d. abet

7. The teacher's encouragement gave Lauren the _____ she needed to do her best.

     a. impetus   b. dearth   c. iota   d. foreboding

8. "Your explanation is _____," the detective said. "The crime could have happened just as you say."

     a. notorious   b. mediocre   c. garrulous   d. plausible

9. Growing conditions were so perfect this year that there was a _____ of tomatoes, causing prices to drop.

     a. knack   b. venture   c. vestige   d. glut

10. Armed forces were able to _____ the revolt and protect the palace.

     a. boost   b. quell   c. jibe   d. rouse

B Circle the correct synonym for each underlined word.

11. make a <u>commitment</u>
    a. contrivance   b. pledge   c. journey   d. tumult

12.   <u>prohibit</u> smoking
    a. ban   b. regret   c. scorn   d. reprove

13. a <u>dire</u> situation
    a. dreadful   b. sensible   c. delightful   d. prosperous

14. <u>opportune</u> time to look for a job
    a. opulent   b. timorous   c. favorable   d. pretentious

15. a well-known <u>adage</u>
    a. malefactor   b. investigator   c. expedition   d. proverb

16. a <u>brawny</u> athlete
    a. charitable   b. impudent   c. muscular   d. uncompromising

17. <u>spurn</u> an offer
    a. refuse   b. provoke   c. savor   d. wheedle

18. an <u>insolent</u> remark
    a. eminent   b. impertinent   c. outmoded   d. irrelevant

19. <u>devise</u> a plan of action
    a. ridicule   b. erase   c. formulate   d. refuse

20. <u>notorious</u> bank robbers
    a. unimportant   b. shrewd   c. loquacious   d. infamous

LESSON 9

Some of the words that you will encounter on pages 94–95 and 97–98 of this lesson appear in bold type in the following poem. Read the poem, and on a separate sheet of paper, answer the question that follows.

> Jed Simmons is such a **gullible** soul,
> He can't tell the truth from a lie.
> His **initial** reaction is always trust,
> Never doubting or asking why.
>
> An **unscrupulous** salesman sold him a car;
> The man was a smooth-talking liar.
> Jed believed he was getting a deal,
> But the car had only one tire.

In previous lessons, you learned how you can often figure out unfamiliar words by combining context clues with your knowledge and experience. How do context clues help you understand what this poem is about?

 LESSON WORDS 1–10: Pronounce the word, spell it, study its meanings, and finish the sentence that follows it.

---

amass (*v.*)   collect for oneself; pile up; **accumulate**; **gather**
ə-'mas

   1. (Scholars, Misers) _____ *amass* a wealth of knowledge.

apprehensive (*adj.*)   fearful about something that might happen;
ˌa-pri-'hen(t)-siv   **uneasy**; **anxious**

   2. We are *apprehensive* when we lead by a (scant, insurmountable) _____ margin.

deplete (*v.*)   empty completely or partially; **drain**; **exhaust**;
di-'plēt   **lessen**

> 3. The long (dry, rainy) _____ spell has almost
>   *depleted* our reservoirs.

enigma (*n.*)   something puzzling or hard to explain; **mystery**;
i-'nig-mə   **riddle**; **puzzle**

> 4. To (a literate, an illiterate) _____ person, a book is
>   an *enigma*.

fathom (*v.*)   get to the bottom of; understand thoroughly;
'fa-thəm   **interpret**; **penetrate**

> 5. It takes (luck, astuteness) _____ to *fathom* an
>   opponent's strategy.

gullible (*adj.*)   easily tricked or cheated; **credulous**; **naive**
'gə-lə-bəl

> 6. *Gullible* people rarely (do, question) _____ what
>   they are told.

imminent (*adj.*)   about to take place; at hand; **impending**;
'i-mə-nənt   **threatening**; **near**

> 7. The jury has (ended, begun) _____ deliberations; a
>   verdict is *imminent*.

increment (*n.*)   something added; **increase**; **addition**; **raise**
'iŋ-krə-mənt

> 8. I was hired at $195 a week, and now I make $220; I got a
>   ($15, $25) _____ *increment*.

initial (*adj.*)   occurring at the beginning; **first**; **introductory**
i-'ni-shəl

> 9. Sally settled for ice cream because there was no rice pud-
>   ding; (ice cream, rice pudding) _____ was her *ini-
>   tial* choice.

lavish (*adj.*)   very generous in giving or spending; **prodigal**;
'la-vish   **profuse**; **unstinting**

> 10. A *lavish* hostess serves (tiny, large) _____ portions.

SENTENCE COMPLETION 1–10: Enter the required lesson words.

1. Our club was so _____ in its spending the past two months that it almost _____**d** the treasury.

2. The smile of Leonardo da Vinci's Mona Lisa remains a(n) _____ despite the efforts of countless viewers to _____ it.

3. P. T. Barnum, who once said, "A sucker is born every minute," knew that people are _____, and he used that knowledge to _____ a fortune.

4. Since new employees can qualify for a(n) _____ every six months, by year's end they may be earning much more than their _____ salary.

5. After the earthquake, many of the region's terrified inhabitants were _____ that another quake was _____.

VOCABULARY IN CONTEXT 1–10: Read the paragraph, and on a separate sheet of paper, answer the questions that follow. Do not repeat any of the underlined words in your answers; use synonyms instead.

Certain subjects can make students <u>apprehensive</u>. Algebra, for example, is an <u>enigma</u> for some students. They can't <u>fathom</u> complex word problems. At the first mention of a test, these students worry that disaster is <u>imminent</u>. However, more often than not, their <u>initial</u> fears prove <u>groundless</u>. They discover that they understand more than they thought they did.

1. What is the main idea of this paragraph?

2. What subject makes you apprehensive? Why? What might you do to calm your fears?

LESSON WORDS 11–20: Pronounce the word, spell it, study its meanings, and finish the sentence that follows it.

legible (*adj.*)   capable of being read; easy to read; **readable**;
'le-jə-bəl   **decipherable**

    11. A (scribbled, typed) _____ message is usually *legible.*

melancholy (*adj.*)   in a gloomy state of mind; **sad**; **depressed**;
'me-lən-ˌkä-lē   **heavyhearted**

    12. A (pickup, downturn) _____ in sales makes merchants *melancholy.*

obligatory (*adj.*)   legally or morally binding; **mandatory**;
ə-'blig-ə-ˌtȯr-ē   **required**

    13. It is *obligatory* for drivers to carry (passengers, identification) _____ .

ordeal (*n.*)   extremely difficult experience that tries one's character
ȯr-'dē(ə)l   or endurance; **trial**; **test**

    14. Living through a (hurricane, sun-shower) _____ is an *ordeal.*

paltry (*adj.*)   of little or no value; **cheap**; **shoddy**; **trivial**;
'pȯl-trē   **picayune**

    15. A few (raindrops, nosebleeds) _____ are a *paltry* excuse for absence.

stalemate (*n.*)   situation in which no action can be taken;
'stā(ə)l-ˌmāt   **deadlock**; **tie**; **draw**

    16. Casualties (soar, plummet) _____ during a *stalemate* in hostilities.

tension (*n.*)   mental or emotional strain; **suspense**; **anxiety**;
'ten(t)-shən   **stress**

    17. *Tension* (mounts, abates) _____ as we approach a crisis.

unscrupulous (*adj.*)   acting without strict regard for what is right;
ˌən-'skrü-pyə-ləs   lacking in moral principles; **unprincipled**;
conscienceless

18. *Unscrupulous* politicians are mainly concerned with their
(personal, community's) _____ welfare.

vicinity (*n.*)   surrounding area or region; **neighborhood**;
və-'si-nə-tē   **locality**

19. Residents in the *vicinity* of the (airport, library)
_____ complain of noise pollution.

vivacious (*adj.*)   full of life and spirits; **lively**; **sprightly**; **active**
və-'vā-shəs

20. *Vivacious* children are not usually (noisy, quiet)
_____ .

SENTENCE COMPLETION 11–20: Enter the required
lesson words from D, above.

---

1. The _____ pearl buyers of La Paz tried to force Kino to
sell his beautiful rare pearl for the _____ sum of 1,500
pesos.

2. Driving to your new house in last night's storm was a(n)
_____ because the roads were flooded, and it was too
dark for street signs to be _____ .

3. The _____ among the residents subsided when the
escaped murderer reported to be in their _____ was
recaptured.

4. Many think it should be _____ for union and management, when they reach a(n) _____, to submit their differences to arbitration.

5. Pam, one of my most _____ friends, has been
_____ ever since she lost her dog.

VOCABULARY IN CONTEXT 11–20: Read the paragraph, and on a separate sheet of paper, answer the questions that follow. Do not repeat any of the underlined words in your answers; use synonyms instead.

Maria was driving in the <u>vicinity</u> of Greenville, when she suddenly realized that she had gotten lost. She pulled over to check her handwritten directions, but they had gotten so crumpled up that they were no longer <u>legible</u>. A knot of <u>tension</u> formed in her stomach. *I'm not going to make it,* she thought. *I'm going to be late for my job interview.* Maria considered what to do next, trying not to let her <u>melancholy</u> mood cloud her judgment.

1. Describe how Maria is feeling.

2. What advice would you give Maria?

SYNONYMS: To avoid repetition, replace the boldfaced word or expression with a synonym from the vocabulary list below.

deplete	mandatory	depressed	initial	accumulate
trial	locality	uneasy	anxiety	comprehend

1. Unless you are in top condition, basketball will quickly **exhaust** your energy; it is an exhausting sport.   1. _____

2. Having to take five examinations in one day is a(n) **trying experience** that Pat hopes never to experience again.   2. _____

3. In the **first** match, you were the first to score.   3. _____

4. If you look tense when you visit a seriously ill patient, you will only add to the **tension** he is having about his health.   4. _____

5. At that restaurant, jackets and ties are **required** for gentlemen, but no one had ever warned Dan of this requirement.

5. _____

6. How did you ever manage to **amass** such a mass of junk?

6. _____

7. Neighbors say that a disturbed stray dog has been seen in this **neighborhood**.

7. _____

8. After our defeat, there was an atmosphere of gloom in the stands; all the fans were **in a gloomy frame of mind**.

8. _____

9. The performers were a bit **apprehensive** before curtain time, but the warmth of the audience soon dispelled their apprehension.

9. _____

10. Champollion was able to **interpret** the Egyptian hieroglyphics, a picture language that had defied interpretation.

10. _____

 ANTONYMS: In the blank space in each sentence below, enter the word most nearly the antonym of the boldfaced word or words. Choose your antonyms from the following list.

| credulous | sprightly | undecipherable | shoddy | prodigal |
| impending | increment | unprincipled | drain | enigma |

1. In a drought, we must be extremely **sparing**, rather than _____, in using water.

2. Not everyone received a(n) _____; some had to take a **cut in pay**.

3. Most of the faculty's signatures were **legible**, but one was _____.

4. Though they seemed to be **acting with a strict regard for what is right and what is wrong**, they were really

   _____ .

5. Exaggerated advertising claims may mislead some _____ people, but not the **astute** shopper.

6. A person who is poor in explaining can make **something not puzzling** seem like a(n) _____ .

7. If we _____ our timber reserves, it will be hard to **replace** them.

8. These puppies are extremely _____ ; only when they are asleep are they **inactive**.

9. The necklace Matilda had lost was really not **valuable**; it was a(n) _____ imitation of an expensive necklace.

10. Before discussing problems that seem **far off in the future**, let us deal with some _____ issues.

 CONCISE WRITING: Express the thought of each sentence in NO MORE THAN FOUR WORDS.

---

1. A work stoppage to force compliance with the employees' demands is about to take place.

   _____

2. A troubleshooter gets to the bottom of things that are puzzling or hard to explain.

   _____

3. The extremely difficult and trying experience that we have been going through is coming to an end.

   _____

4. Has there ever been a time when you were in a gloomy state of mind?

   _____

5. The person that you have allied yourself with does not seem to have a strict regard for what is right and proper.

_____

6. Those who were new to the job were fearful that something might happen.

_____

J   **VOCABULARY SKILL BUILDER**

Word Parts: Prefixes and Suffixes

In Lessons 6 and 8 (pages 64 and 84), you learned the meaning of a number of prefixes and suffixes. Here are some others. The examples are vocabulary words or synonyms that appeared in this lesson or a previous lesson.

Prefix	Meaning	Example
in-	"not"; "the opposite of"	insufficient
dis-	"not"; "the opposite of"	disheartened

Suffix	Meaning	Example
-ful	"full of"; "characterized by"; "tending to"	dreadful
-ous	"full of"; "characterized by"	famous

Exercises

Each of the following words appears as a lesson word or a synonym in this lesson or in an earlier lesson. Circle the prefix and/or suffix in each word. (Some prefixes and suffixes may be from previous lessons.) Then use the word in a sentence. If you need help, check a dictionary.

1. disregard

_____

2. imperfection

_____

3. unstinting

_____

4. vigorous

_____

5. watchful

_____

6. decipherable

_____

 WRITING SKILL BUILDER

Using Word Bridges

Transitional words and phrases act as bridges, connecting ideas and supporting information. Here are some examples. What others can you think of?

Transitional Word or Phrase	Purpose
for example, for instance	Gives an example

> _Example:_ Some chores are worse than others. **For example**, I'd rather take out the garbage than clean the cat's litter box.

Transitional Word or Phrase	Purpose
also, in addition, too	Adds information

> _Example:_ Michael is a talented writer. **In addition**, he is an outstanding math student.

first, second, third (and so on);   Shows sequence or time
**next; finally; after; before;
during; meanwhile; then**

Example: **First**, the basement pipe froze. **Then** it
cracked, and water came pouring out.
Meanwhile, the family was upstairs,
unaware of what had happened.

Activity

Think of a noteworthy or amusing incident that you either read about
or observed. Write a paragraph or two describing the incident and
explaining why you chose to write about it. Use transitional words
and phrases to connect ideas and supporting information. In your
writing, include at least two of the words that you learned in this lesson. Write your paragraph(s) on a separate sheet of paper.

LESSON 10

Lesson Preview

Some of the words that you will encounter on pages 105–106 and 108–109 of this lesson appear in bold type in the following paragraphs. Read the paragraphs, and on a separate sheet of paper, answer the questions that follow.

> The carpenter's explanation for the broken window was **preposterous**, and Ms. Solomon did not believe it for a second. Clearly, the man felt no **obligation** to tell the truth.
>
> "You're going to have to **reimburse** me for getting the window repaired," Ms. Solomon said angrily. "Your conduct is **appalling**," she added. "I **deplore** your lack of honesty."

Is Ms. Solomon pleased with the carpenter? How do you know?

LESSON WORDS 1–10: Pronounce the word, spell it, study its meanings, and finish the sentence that follows it.

---

adorn (*v.*) add beauty to; make more attractive; **decorate**;
ə-'dȯrn   **embellish**; **beautify**

1. The room is beautiful; (cobwebs, paintings) _____ *adorn* the walls.

appalling (*adj.*) filled with horror, shock, or dismay; **frightful**;
ə-'pȯl-iŋ   **shocking**

2. There was (great, no) _____ suffering; conditions were *appalling*.

barren (*adj.*) producing little or no vegetation; incapable of
'bar-ən   producing offspring; **unproductive**; **sterile**

3. *Barren* fields yield (bumper, meager) _____ crops.

105

buffoon (n.)   person given to joking, clowning, or playing pranks;
(,)bə-'fün   **clown; zany**

  4. The circus *buffoons* make children (cry, laugh)
  _____ .

congenial (adj.)   having the same tastes and temperament;
kən-'jē-nē-əl, or   **friendly; sociable**
kən-'jēn-yəl

  5. *Congenial* people (rarely, never) _____ disagree.

corroborate (v.)   support with evidence; **confirm; substantiate;**
kə-'rä-bə-,rāt   **verify**

  6. Rumor becomes truth (before, after) _____ it is
  corroborated.

curtail (v.)   cut back; **shorten; lessen; abbreviate; reduce**
(,)kər-'tā(ə)l

  7. Service is *curtailed* today; (fewer, more) _____
  buses are running.

deplore (v.)   regret strongly; disapprove of; feel grief for; **lament;**
di-'plȯr   **bewail**

  8. We *deplore* your conduct. Why were you (unkempt,
  uncivil) _____?

enhance (v.)   add or contribute to; **increase; augment;**
in-'han(t)s   **improve; intensify**

  9. Spices *enhance* the (flavor, spoilage) _____ of food.

festive (adj.)   of or suited to a feast or festival; **joyful; merry;**
'fes-tiv   **jovial**

  10. On a *festive* occasion, let us not be (melancholy, merry)
  _____ .

SENTENCE COMPLETION 1–10: Enter the required lesson words.

1. Both the North and the South deeply _____**d** the _____ bloodshed in the Battle of Gettysburg, in which 50,000 soldiers lost their lives.

2. Joke and clown, if you wish, at _____ gatherings, like parties, but in an employment interview don't behave like a(n) _____ .

3. Though the charges that the candidate is an alcoholic have yet to be _____**d**, they have certainly not _____**d** his reputation.

4. Our neighbor Rose was going to _____ her visit to the playground, but she changed her mind when her children found _____ playmates there.

5. Here and there, a flowering cactus _____**s** the otherwise _____ desert.

 VOCABULARY IN CONTEXT 1–10: Read the paragraph, and on a separate sheet of paper, answer the questions that follow. Do not repeat any of the underlined words in your answers; use synonyms instead.

Using paint and decorations, Lisa transformed her bedroom from dull and dreary to bright and lively. First, she applied vivid colors to the walls to enhance the cheeriness of the room. Then she adorned the walls with colorful pictures and posters. When she finished, the bedroom had taken on an almost festive look, which made her feel happy.

1. In Lesson 7 (page 74), you read how writers sometimes contrast people, places, or things. Explain the contrast in this paragraph. Be specific.

2. What else might Lisa do to "enhance the cheeriness" of her bedroom?

LESSON WORDS 11–20: Pronounce the word, spell it, study its meanings, and finish the sentence that follows it.

malicious (*adj.*)   full of malice (ill will); desirous of doing mischief
mə-'li-shəs   or making others suffer; **spiteful**; **malevolent**

11. A *malicious* fan pelted the visitors with (flowers, eggs)
_____.

meritorious (*adj.*)   worthy of honor; **praiseworthy**;
‚mer-ə-'tōr-ē-əs   **commendable**; **laudable**; **deserving**

12. *Meritorious* deeds should not be (rewarded, ignored)
_____.

minimize (*v.*)   make (something or someone) appear as
'mi-nə-‚mīz   unimportant as possible; **belittle**; **disparage**;
decry

13. By boasting that she had done (nothing, everything)
_____, she *minimized* our contribution to the
show.

obligation (*n.*)   something one is bound to do; **duty**;
‚ä-blə-'gā-shən   **responsibility**

14. It is a tenant's *obligation* to (pay, collect) _____
rent.

preposterous (*adj.*)   completely contrary to nature, reason, or
pri-'päs-t(ə-)rəs   common sense; utterly foolish; **absurd**;
senseless; **ridiculous**

15. It is *preposterous* to claim to be (invincible, vulnerable)
_____.

procrastinate (*v.*)   defer action; habitually put off the doing of
prə-'kras-tə-‚nāt   something that should be done; **delay**;
dawdle; **postpone**

16. I was far (behind, ahead) _____ because I had
procrastinated.

reimburse (*v.*)   make repayment (to someone) for expenses or
,re-əm-'bərs   losses incurred; **repay**; **recompense**;
compensate

17. Ann *reimbursed* me for the things I had (bought, sold)
_____ for her.

skinflint (*n.*)   one who is very hard and grasping in money matters;
'skin-,flint   **miser**; **tightwad**; **pinchpenny**

18. *Skinflints,* as a rule, tip very (lavishly, sparingly)
_____ .

toxic (*adj.*)   affected by or acting as a poison; **poisonous**;
'täk-sik   **venomous**

19. The (honey, sting) _____ of a bee can have a *toxic*
effect.

zeal (*n.*)   intense enthusiasm; impassioned eagerness; **ardor**;
'zē(ə)l   **fervor**; **passion**

20. I was (chided, praised) _____ for a lack of *zeal* in
doing my chores.

SENTENCE COMPLETION 11–20: Enter the required
lesson words from D, above.

---

1. Donna was applauded for her acting by everyone except a(n)
_____ rival who tried to _____ her
achievement.

2. Since Gulliver had just rendered highly _____ service
to the kingdom of Lilliput, it was _____ that he should
be accused of treason.

3. If you incur any expenses in doing Randy a favor, you may be
sure he will quickly _____ you; he is no
_____ .

4. Let us act now to stop the illegal dumping of _____
wastes; if we _____, the situation will only get worse.

5. The rescue squad deserves praise for its speedy response in emergencies, and for the skill and _____ with which it performs its _____s.

VOCABULARY IN CONTEXT 11–20: Read the paragraph, and on a separate sheet of paper, answer the questions that follow. Do not repeat any of the underlined words in your answers; use synonyms instead.

My New Year's resolution this year is to stop <u>procrastinating</u>. I used to <u>minimize</u> the importance of taking prompt action. However, I've learned that putting tasks off is a bad habit. I have an <u>obligation</u> to myself to get things done on time. In the past, I would begin a project with great <u>zeal</u>. But after a while, I would fall into my old I'll-get-to-it-tomorrow routine. Well, no more! From now on, no more procrastinating! I'm going to put my resolution into practice next week. Or, maybe the week after. I'll see.

1. What is the narrator's plan? Why is the narrator making this plan?

2. Do you think the narrator will succeed in the resolution? Why or why not?

SYNONYMS: To avoid repetition, replace the boldfaced word with a synonym from the vocabulary list below.

bewail	poisonous	substantiate	jovial	frightful
recompense	spiteful	responsibility	ardor	laudable

1. Lead, a highly **toxic** metal, was used extensively in water pipes in the olden days when its toxicity was unknown.   1. _____

2. Some say Joe's idea is **meritorious**, but I see no merit in it.   2. _____

3. We are appalled by the bad news; the situation is **appalling**.   3. _____

4. At first, we zealously supported our
   legislator, but when he was convicted
   of taking bribes, our **zeal** for him
   plummeted.   4. _____

5. Witnesses were called to **corroborate**
   the defendant's claim, but the scant
   evidence they offered fell far short
   of corroboration.   5. _____

6. Though some in the past have been
   reimbursed for their expenses,
   I have no assurance that I will receive
   any reimbursement.   6. _____**d**

7. Your fellow employees are not
   obliged to do your work for you;
   that is your **obligation**.   7. _____

8. Let's not **deplore** our fate; it is not
   so deplorable as we think.   8. _____

9. Although you insist that your coach
   is **malicious**, we see no malice in
   her whatsoever.   9. _____

10. People who attend a festival are
    usually in a **festive** mood.   10. _____

 ANTONYMS: In the blank in each sentence below, enter
the word most nearly the antonym of the boldfaced word
or words. Choose your antonyms from the following list.

| confirm | augment | abbreviate | absurd | sterile |
| sociable | malevolent | venomous | embellish | commendable |

1. Not all of the suggestions were **sensible**; a few were utterly

   _____.

2. Unlike garter snakes, which are **nonpoisonous**, rattlesnakes
   are dangerously _____.

3. Horses are **capable of producing offspring**, but mules are

   _____.

4. Graffiti **mar the appearance of** a wall; they surely do not
   _____ it.

5. Othello failed to see that Iago, who seemed like a person **of
   good will**, was in fact _____ .

6. So far, there is little to **contradict** or _____ the exis-
   tence of other worlds like ours in the universe.

7. Our guests had intended to **extend** their visit, but inclement
   weather compelled them to _____ it.

8. By its conduct, a nation can either _____ or **decrease**
   its prestige.

9. Keisha reports that her colleagues in the office are quite
   _____ , except for one or two who seem
   uncongenial.

10. Benedict Arnold must have been riled when his superiors con-
    sidered his outstandingly _____ battlefield record
    undeserving of promotion.

CONCISE WRITING: Express the thought of each sentence
in NO MORE THAN FOUR WORDS.

---

1. Why are you in the habit of putting off the doing of what has to
   be done now to some indefinite time in the future?

   _____

2. She makes the hardships that she has been going through seem
   as unimportant as possible.

   _____

3. In matters that have to do with money, he is very hard and
   grasping.

   _____

4. The stories that they have been telling are full of horror, shock,
   and dismay.

   _____

5. Stay away from those who are desirous of making other people suffer or doing mischief.

_____

6. Do your teammates have the same temperament and tastes that you have?

_____

J   VOCABULARY SKILL BUILDER

Word Parts: Verb Suffixes

Some suffixes are used to form verbs. The three suffixes shown below all mean "to make" or "to cause to be."

Suffix	Example
-en	weak + **-en** = weaken
-fy	simple + **-fy** = simplify
-ize	popular + **-ize** = popularize

Exercises

1. Each of the following words appears as a lesson word or a synonym in this lesson. Circle the suffix in each word. Then use the word in a sentence. If you need help, check a dictionary.

   a. intensify

   _____

   b. shorten

   _____

   c. minimize

   _____

d. verify

_____

e. lessen

_____

f. beautify

_____

2. *Verify* comes from the Latin word *verus,* meaning "true." How does the combination of this root and the suffix **-fy** suggest the meaning of *verify*?

_____

 WRITING SKILL BUILDER

More Word Bridges

In the previous lesson (pages 103–104), you saw how transitional words and phrases act as bridges. Here are some other examples of word bridges.

Transitional Word or Phrase	Purpose
because of, as a result, therefore, consequently	State an effect or result

    Example: Schools were closed **because of** the storm.

Transitional Word or Phrase	Purpose
however, on the other hand, but, although, even though	Make a comparison or signal a change in focus

    Example: Brendan and Daniel are both excellent basketball players. **However**, Brendan is nearly four inches taller than Daniel.

especially, in fact, most   Add emphasis
important, above all

> *Example:* The Grand Canyon is an impressive sight.
> **In fact**, it's one of the most memorable
> places in the United States.

Activity

Think of a noteworthy place that you have visited. Write a paragraph or two describing the place and explaining why you chose to write about it. Use transitional words and phrases to connect ideas and supporting information. In your writing, include at least two of the words that you learned in this lesson. Write your paragraph(s) on a separate sheet of paper.

LESSON 11

Lesson Preview

Some of the words that you will encounter on pages 116–117 and
119–120 of this lesson appear in bold type in the following poem.
Read the poem, and on a separate sheet of paper, answer the questions that follow.

> "There are ants in my kitchen!" Ann cried into the phone.
> "You must come at once," she said in a desperate tone.
> "My need is **urgent**, and I will be **irate**,
> If you don't bring your sprays, your traps, and your bait."
>
> The exterminator said, "**Remove** them we will.
> We'll **eliminate** them all, and send you the bill.
> Our **function** is clear, and our methods are many.
> By the time we are through, you will not see any!"

How many speakers are there in this poem? Who are they? What is
this poem about?

 LESSON WORDS 1–10: Pronounce the word, spell it,
study its meanings, and finish the sentence that follows it.

---

allot (*v.*) give as a share or portion; **assign**; **allocate**; **apportion**
ə-'lät

1. Since only twelve minutes were left, each of the three candidates was *allotted* (four, three) _____ minutes for a
   summary.

appropriate (*v.*) take without permission for one's own use;
ə-'prō-prē-ˌāt **seize**; **annex**

2. The law of the jungle (forbids, permits) _____ the
   strong to *appropriate* the property of the weak.

116

dialogue (*n.*) exchange of ideas; **conversation**; **discussion**;
'dī-ə-ˌläg **chat**

   3. We (greeted, ignored) _____ each other; there was
      no *dialogue*.

dispensable (*adj.*) capable of being done without; **nonessential**;
di-'spen(t)-sə-bəl **unimportant**

   4. In (nonsmoking, smoking) _____ areas, ashtrays
      are *dispensable*.

eliminate (*v.*) get rid of; **remove**; **exclude**
i-'li-mə-ˌnāt

   5. If tolls are *eliminated*, traffic will (slow down, speed up)
      _____ .

entice (*v.*) lead on by exciting hope or desire; **tempt**; **lure**;
in-'tīs **inveigle**

   6. (Pleasant, Obnoxious) _____ odors *enticed* us into
      the kitchen.

expedite (*v.*) speed up the process of; **hasten**; **accelerate**
'ek-spə-ˌdīt

   7. Order by (phone, mail) _____ to *expedite* delivery.

fracas (*n.*) noisy, disorderly disturbance or fight; **altercation**;
'frā-kəs **brawl**; **row**

   8. When we have no umpire, there is (more, less)
      _____ likelihood of a *fracas*.

frugal (*adj.*) avoiding waste; not spending unnecessarily; **sparing**;
'frü-gəl **economical**; **thrifty**

   9. One has to be *frugal* to live on a (meager, generous)
      _____ income.

function (*n.*) action proper to a person or thing; **purpose**; **duty**;
'fəŋ(k)-shən **role**

   10. The *function* of a heater is to (lower, elevate)
      _____ the temperature.

SENTENCE COMPLETION 1–10: Enter the required lesson words.

1. Gail's _____ at the department store is to _____ the application process for credit cards.

2. One way for the government to reduce expenses is to _____ all _____ items from next year's budget.

3. A latecomer's attempt to _____ someone's seat in the rear of the auditorium touched off a brief but heated _____ .

4. After surrounding his hideout, the police _____**d** the armed convict into a(n) _____, and shortly afterward he surrendered peacefully.

5. Be _____ in serving the ice cream, or some of us may not get any; _____ no more than one scoop per person until everyone has been served.

VOCABULARY IN CONTEXT 1–10: Read the paragraph, and on a separate sheet of paper, answer the questions that follow. Do not repeat any of the underlined words in your answers; use synonyms instead.

If you have an argument with a friend, it's important for the two of you to talk things over. Without honest <u>dialogue</u>, your disagreement cannot be settled. To <u>expedite</u> matters, try to <u>eliminate</u> emotions and focus only on facts. <u>Allot</u> each other time to speak without interruption. Listen carefully, and try to understand the other person's point of view.

1. What is the main idea of this paragraph?

2. What else could two friends do to expedite the settlement of a disagreement?

LESSON WORDS 11–20: Pronounce the word, spell it, study its meanings, and finish the sentence that follows it.

irate (*adj.*)   arising from or characterized by anger; **enraged**;
ī-'rāt   **furious**

11. His *irate* reply shows he was (puzzled, offended) _____ by her question.

lackluster (*adj.*)   lacking brilliance or vitality; **dull**; **uninspired**;
'lak-,ləs-tər   **mediocre**

12. Merchants are (impressed, unhappy) _____ with *lackluster* profits.

mimic (*n.*)   one who mimics or imitates; **imitator**; **impersonator**
'mi-mik

13. Some *mimics* excel in (imitating, correcting) _____ the speech of celebrities.

omnipotent (*adj.*)   having unlimited or very great power or
äm-'ni-pə-tənt   authority; **all-powerful**; **almighty**

14. The Greeks knew there was (a, no) _____ limit to what they could do, but they considered their gods *omnipotent*.

quandary (*n.*)   state of uncertainty as to what to do: **dilemma**;
'kwän-d(ə-)rē   **predicament**

15. Experts who give (conflicting, detailed) _____ advice put us in a *quandary*.

ravenous (*adj.*)   extremely eager for food; **famished**; **voracious**
'rav-(ə-)nəs

16. The *ravenous* guests devoured everything but the (ripe, artificial) _____ fruit.

slacken (v.)   make less active; slow up; **relax**; **untighten**;
'sla-kən   **moderate**

    17. Accidents (rise, decline) _____ when the enforce-
ment of traffic rules is *slackened.*

unnerve (v.)   cause to lose courage or confidence; **upset**; **fluster**;
ˌən-'nərv   **disconcert**

    18. The shouts of hostile fans so *unnerved* Paula that she
(scored, missed) _____ an easy basket.

urgent (adj.)   requiring immediate attention; **pressing**;
'ər-jənt   **compelling**; **grave**

    19. When reservoirs are nearly (empty, full) _____,
there is *urgent* need for conservation.

vulnerable (adj.)   open to attack, injury, or damage; **assailable**;
'vəl-n(ə-)rə-bəl   **exposed**

    20. If streams overflow, homes on (high, low) _____
ground may be *vulnerable* to flooding.

 SENTENCE COMPLETION 11–20: Enter the required
lesson words from D, above.

---

1. The plight of the earthquake survivors is so _____ that
we must not _____ our efforts to help them.

2. It is a dangerous mistake for champions to think they are
_____; overconfidence may make them _____
.

3. Who would not be _____d on an Arctic night to hear
the howls of _____ wolves getting closer and closer?

4. The director was so _____ over the band's
_____ performance that she scheduled an extra
rehearsal for the next day.

5. You would be in a(n) _____ if you tried to identify the mockingbird by its song because it is a gifted _____ of other birds.

VOCABULARY IN CONTEXT 11–20: Read the paragraph, and on a separate sheet of paper, answer the questions that follow. Do not repeat any of the underlined words in your answers; use synonyms instead.

In nature, the power of the hunter is often far greater than that of the hunted. The fierce cats of Africa and Asia, for example, seem almost <u>omnipotent</u> when compared to the animals they hunt. Imagine a sheep pursued by a <u>ravenous</u> tiger. How <u>vulnerable</u> must that sheep feel when faced with those claws and teeth! The mere sight of a 500-pound tiger would be enough to <u>unnerve</u> most living creatures.

1. What is the main idea of this paragraph?

2. Do you agree or disagree with the following analogy? Why or why not?

   CAT : MOUSE as TIGER : SHEEP

SYNONYMS: To avoid repetition, replace the boldfaced word or expression with a synonym from the vocabulary list below.

---

inveigle	seize	economical	disconcert	enraged
pressing	relax	uninspiring	nonessential	dilemma

1. If the decorations are **dispensable**, let's dispense with them.

   1. _____

2. It is inappropriate for any one to **appropriate** vacant property.

   2. _____

3. Your grip on the bat is too tight; **untighten** it a bit.

   3. _____

4. Some people are uncertain about
   so many things that they are always
   in a(n) **state of uncertainty**.   4. _____

5. Parking is truly a(n) **urgent** matter,
   but there are problems of much
   greater urgency confronting us.   5. _____

6. A nervous person is easily **unnerved**
   by an unexpected change.   6. _____**ed**

7. Critics look for excellence, not
   mediocrity; they steer the public
   away from **mediocre** productions.   7. _____

8. The misleading offer was so enticing that
   many were **enticed** into accepting it.   8. _____**d**

9. When our health is at risk, we spare
   no expense to get well; otherwise,
   we are **sparing** with our money.   9. _____

10. The captain would become **furious**
    when his ire was aroused, so the crew
    tried not to infuriate him.   10. _____

ANTONYMS: In the blank space in each sentence below, enter the word most nearly the antonym of the boldfaced word or words. Choose your antonyms from the following list.

| unassailable | moderate | inspired | appropriate | calm |
| indispensable | lavish | restore | powerless | repel |

1. The defendants had been _____ during the trial, but
   when they heard the verdict, they became **irate**.

2. Does violence in a movie _____ you, or does it **lure**
   you to keep watching?

3. The castle was _____, but the rest of the place was
   open to attack.

4. With limited resources, we must be **frugal**; we cannot afford to
   be _____.

5. In totalitarian states, rulers are **omnipotent** and subjects are
_____.

6. Don't expect an actress to give a(n) _____ performance
if she has to work with a **dull** script.

7. Some want us to **speed up** our pace; others say we should
_____ it.

8. Leave **nonessential** equipment behind; take along only what is
_____.

9. None of the items **eliminated** from the budget have been
_____**d**.

10. Did he **take** your bicycle **with permission**, or did he simply
_____ it?

CONCISE WRITING: Express the thought of each sentence
in NO MORE THAN FOUR WORDS.

---

1. All of a sudden, the exchange of ideas that they had been having
came to an abrupt end.

_____

2. Who is the individual who started that noisy, disorderly
disturbance?

_____

3. The situation that we find ourselves in is one that requires immediate attention.

_____

4. There seemed to be no limit whatsoever to the power of the
invaders.

_____

5. Someone took the racket that belongs to Cynthia without bothering to ask her permission.

6. The boos that were emitted caused us to lose confidence in ourselves.

 VOCABULARY SKILL BUILDER

Context Clues: Cause and Effect

A *cause* produces an *effect*, or result. For example, a bat hitting a baseball (cause) makes the ball fly through the air (effect). Identifying causes and effects can help you figure out the meaning of unfamiliar words.

> *Example:* Scrubbing with soap and water eliminated the dirt and left the floor spotless.
>
> *Context clues:* "Scrubbing with soap and water" is the cause. Its effect or result was a spotless floor—a floor from which the dirt had been *eliminated*.

Exercises

On a separate sheet of paper, explain how cause and effect can help you figure out the meaning of each underlined word.

1. Emily was so ravenous that she ate five slices of pizza.

2. Because the patient's condition was urgent, the doctor examined him at once.

3. Their frugal spending habits enabled the Patels to save a large amount of money.

From Paragraph to Essay

An *essay* is a composition of two or more paragraphs dealing with a particular topic from the writer's viewpoint. An essay should have a clear central idea. Every paragraph in the essay should relate to that idea. Just as the supporting information in a paragraph develops the topic sentence, so should the supporting paragraphs in an essay develop the central idea.

Activity

Do you think the voting age should be lowered to 16? Why or why not?

Write an essay of at least two paragraphs expressing your point of view. Be sure that your essay has a clear central idea and that every paragraph relates to that idea. Support your position with specific reasons, facts, or examples. In your essay, use at least two of the words that you have learned in this lesson. Write your essay on a separate sheet of paper.

LESSON 12

Lesson Preview

Lesson Preview

Some of the words that you will encounter on pages 126–127 and 129–130 of this lesson appear in bold type in the following paragraph. Read the paragraph, and on a separate sheet of paper, answer the questions that follow.

> Professor's Moriarity's **intent** was to create a working time travel machine. However, I **anticipated** problems from the very start. As his assistant, I knew that building such a machine would be a long and **laborious** undertaking. I also knew that his **outlandish** idea was nothing more than a **vivid** dream. I tried to be gentle and **tactful** in telling him that, but the professor would not listen. Instead, he climbed into the finished machine, turned a few knobs—and abruptly *disappeared*. At that point, I began to wonder if maybe I had judged the professor unfairly.

Who is the narrator in this paragraph? At the end, why does the narrator think that he may have "judged the professor unfairly"?

LESSON WORDS 1–10: Pronounce the word, spell it, study its meanings, and finish the sentence that follows it.

---

affection (*n.*)   liking or attachment for a person or thing;
ə-'fek-shən   **fondness; devotion**

1. My *affection* for the dog kept me from (stroking, striking) _____ it.

anticipate (*v.*)   give advance thought or treatment to; **expect;**
an-'ti-sə-,pāt   **foresee**

2. Let's get to the game (five, thirty) _____ minutes early because I *anticipate* trouble in finding a parking space.

coerce (*v.*)   force without regard for one's wishes; **compel**;
kō-'ərs   **constrain**

    3. We were not *coerced;* we signed (involuntarily, willingly)

        ——————— .

copious (*adj.*)   large in quantity or number; **abundant; plentiful;**
'kō-pē-əs   **ample**

    4. Potato prices (soar, plummet) ——————— when there is
       a *copious* supply.

dismal (*adj.*)   showing or causing gloom or misery; **dreary**;
'diz-məl   **cheerless**

    5. Our spirits were (depressed, lifted) ——————— by the
       dismal weather.

dominant (*adj.*)   conspicuously prominent; **commanding**;
'dä-mə-nənt   **preeminent; outstanding**

    6. The *dominant* team in the league has not (lost, won)
       ——————— a game.

effect (*n.*)   something traceable to a cause; **result; consequence**;
i-'fekt   **outcome**

    7. One *effect* of heavy rains is (higher, lower) ———————
       reservoir levels.

intent (*n.*)   state of mind with which something is done; **purpose**;
in-'tent   **design; aim**

    8. Murder committed (with, without) ——————— *intent*
       cannot be considered accidental.

jeopardize (*v.*)   put in jeopardy (danger); **endanger; imperil**;
'je-pər-ˌdīz   **compromise**

    9. Our (lavish, frugal) ——————— use of natural resources
       jeopardizes the welfare of future generations.

laborious (*adj.*)   involving much hard work; **arduous; difficult**;
lə-'bȯr-ē-əs   **strenuous**

    10. Computers make record keeping (more, less)
        ——————— *laborious.*

SENTENCE COMPLETION 1–10: Enter the required lesson words.

1. The team's _____ record of two wins in its last eleven games _____s its chances of getting into the play-offs.

2. By _____ effort, country folk are able to amass a(n) _____ supply of firewood for the winter.

3. When sports stars who are friends compete against each other, all _____ between them is usually suppressed; winning is the _____ concern.

4. It was certainly not the manager's _____ to help the robbers; they _____d him into opening the safe.

5. When Midas begged the gods that everything he touched might turn to gold, he did not _____ the _____ this would have on his ability to eat.

VOCABULARY IN CONTEXT 1–10: Read the paragraph, and on a separate sheet of paper, answer the questions that follow. Do not repeat any of the underlined words in your answers; use synonyms instead.

Countless novels and short stories describe one-sided romances. In a typical tale, a lovestruck young man expresses his undying <u>affection</u> for a beautiful woman, only to be turned away. Such rejection leaves the man in <u>dismal</u> spirits. He may even shed <u>copious</u> tears as he tries to think of some way to <u>coerce</u> the woman to love him. But, alas, in the end he learns the hard truth: love cannot be forced.

1. Paraphrase the paragraph.

2. Think of a story you've read or a movie or TV show you've seen in which one character rejects another. What <u>effects</u> did the rejection have?

LESSON WORDS 11–20: Pronounce the word, spell it, study its meanings, and finish the sentence that follows it.

opinionated (*adj.*)　holding unreasonably to one's own opinions or
ə-'pin-yə-,nā-təd　　to preconceived notions; **prejudiced**;
　　　　　　　　　　biased; **stubborn**

    11. *Opinionated* persons are (loath, prone) _____ to modify their views.

option (*n.*)　power or right of choosing; something that may be or is
'äp-shən　　chosen; **choice**; **selection**

    12. If a sale is marked "final," the customer (loses, gets) _____ the *option* of returning the merchandise for a refund.

outlandish (*adj.*)　very odd; **strange**; **peculiar**; **bizarre**
,aùt-'lan-dish

    13. Their *outlandish* manners are sure to (escape, gain) _____ notice.

pact (*n.*)　agreement between persons or nations; **compact**;
'pakt　　**covenant**; **treaty**

    14. *Pacts* between (congenial, distrustful) _____ neighbors tend to endure.

prompt (*v.*)　cause (someone) to do something; **incite**; **spur**;
'präm(p)t　　**induce**

    15. Poor reviews of a film *prompt* moviegoers to (view, shun) _____ it.

refute (*v.*)　prove to be erroneous; **contradict**; **disprove**; **rebut**
ri-'fyüt

    16. (Hearsay, Fact) _____ cannot be *refuted*.

repast (*n.*)   food and drink; **meal**; **dinner**; **feast**
ri-'past

    17. The Thanksgiving *repast* consisted of seven (pages, courses)
    _____ .

tactful (*adj.*)   having a keen sense of what to say or do to maintain
'takt-fəl   good will and avoid giving offense; **adroit**; **clever**;
                    diplomatic

    18. (Ambassadors, Goalies) _____are not expected to
    be tactful.

vain (*adj.*)   of no avail; **useless**; **futile**; **unproductive**
'vān

    19. It is *vain* for us to think we are (vulnerable, omnipotent)
    _____ .

vivid (*adj.*)   presenting the appearance of life; **lively**; **colorful**;
'vi-vəd   **graphic**

    20. The fruit in the painting is so *vivid* that it looks (artificial, edi-
    ble) _____ .

SENTENCE COMPLETION 11–20: Enter the required
lesson words from D, above.

---

  1. Audrey is confident that by being _____ she can
    _____ Oscar's arguments without hurting his feelings.

  2. I have keenly _____ memories of the truly delicious
    _____**s** Grandma used to serve when we visited her.

  3. At a Halloween party, you can appear in the most
    _____ costume, with no possibility that it will
    _____ people to question your sanity.

  4. The employees have two _____**s**: either to accept the
    _____ the mediators have proposed, or to go on strike.

  5. Our attempts to reason with your _____ cousin proved
    _____; we got nowhere.

VOCABULARY IN CONTEXT 11–20: Read the paragraph, and on a separate sheet of paper, answer the questions that follow. Do not repeat any of the underlined words in your answers; use synonyms instead.

Food critics are like movie reviewers, except that they review restaurants instead of films. These highly <u>opinionated</u> individuals visit restaurants, sample the foods, and then write <u>vivid</u> accounts of what they liked and what they did not. The critics make little effort to be <u>tactful</u>. Rather, they evaluate their <u>repast</u> as if it were a used car, pointing out every defect they can find. The reviews they write have great power. Their words <u>prompt</u> hungry diners either to visit a restaurant or to avoid it.

1. Paraphrase the paragraph.

2. If you were a food critic and had the <u>option</u> to visit any restaurant, which one would you choose? Why?

SYNONYMS: To avoid repetition, replace the boldfaced word with a synonym from the vocabulary list below.

---

bizarre	prejudiced	covenant	graphic	compromise
constrain	diplomatic	preeminent	refute	design

1. The business decline has put the company into a dangerous financial position and **endangered** the future of its employees.   1. _____ **d**

2. Learn to be **tactful**; avoid making tactless remarks.   2. _____

3. She did not embarrass us intentionally; that was not her **intent**.   3. _____

4. Her **lively** details made the incident come to life.   4. _____

5. In the rebuttal, debaters have a chance to **rebut** their opponents' arguments.   5. _____

6. When he is wrong about a person,
   he alters his opinion; he is not
   opinionated.   6. _____

7. Shakespeare was the **dominant**
   literary figure of his time; he
   dominated the era.   7. _____

8. What a strange excuse! I never have
   heard of anything so **strange**.   8. _____

9. There was no compulsion; no one
   was **compelled** to contribute.   9. _____**ed**

10. Most observers agree that some of
    those who signed the **agreement**
    are not living up to its terms.   10. _____

 ANTONYMS: In the blank space in each sentence below, enter the word most nearly the antonym of the boldfaced word or words. Choose your antonyms from the following list.

---

spur	option	productive	everyday	coldness
expect	malevolent	scarce	effortless	cheerful

1. In spite of the depressingly **dismal** outlook, they seemed

   _____.

2. Before, we had absolutely **no choice** at all; now we have a(n)

   _____.

3. Sometimes a tactless remark can turn **affection** into

   _____.

4. The wooden horse seemed to the Trojans like a gift **with good
   intent**, but those who were making the gift were, of course,

   _____.

5. Huge jackpots _____ some to buy lottery tickets, but
   they **do not induce** others to part with a penny.

6. Putting aside our _____ clothes, we donned
   outlandish costumes for the masquerade.

7. You _____ed her party to be a success; we **did not anticipate** it.

8. With the proper tools, a **laborious** task can be almost

   _____ .

9. Job opportunities are **abundant** in good times but

   _____ in a depression.

10. Their attempts to solve the enigma were _____, but mine proved **futile**.

CONCISE WRITING: Express the thought of each sentence in NO MORE THAN FOUR WORDS.

---

1. Janet proved that the statement that you made was in error.

   _____

2. In spite of all logic and reason, Tom held firmly to his own pre-conceived ideas and opinions.

   _____

3. The person who advises them has a keen sense of what to say and do to maintain good will and to avoid giving offense.

   _____

4. The attempts that I made turned out to be of no avail.

   _____

5. We gave advance thought to the problems that we would face.

   _____

6. The small routine jobs that have to be done on a farm involve a great deal of hard work.

   _____

| J | **VOCABULARY SKILL BUILDER** |

Connotation and Denotation

A word's *denotation* is its literal meaning—the definition you would find in a dictionary. Many words also have a *connotation*—a meaning that is implied or suggested. A connotation may be positive or negative, favorable or unfavorable.

Here is an example. The word *horde* (a lesson word in Lesson 3) has a number of synonyms, such as *crowd, mob, throng,* and *multitude.* These synonyms have similar denotations but different connotations.

Compare the sentences below. What mental image do the underlined words give you?

A crowd of people lined up to buy movie tickets.

A mob of shoppers searched the mall for holiday sales.

Mob has a negative or unfavorable connotation. Of course, not every word has a particular connotation. *Crowd,* for example, is a neutral word.

Here's another example. The following words all share the same basic denotation, but they have different connotations: *dog, pooch, puppy, mutt, hound.* Which of these words have a positive connotation? A negative connotation? Which are neutral?

Exercises

For each pair of words below, first write the denotation that they have in common. Then explain how the two words differ in their connotation. Most of these words come from earlier lessons. If you need help, check a dictionary.

1. frugal, cheap

_____

_____

2. discussion, chat

_____

_____

3. invention, gadget

_____

_____

4. smart, shrewd

_____

_____

 **WRITING SKILL BUILDER**

Essay Structure

In the previous lesson, you read that an essay should have a clear central idea, and every paragraph in the essay should relate to that idea. Most essays have three parts: an introduction, a body, and a conclusion. The introduction introduces the topic and states the central idea. The body supports and develops that idea. The conclusion brings the essay to a close.

Activity

Some people believe that art and music should be required subjects at school. Others disagree. What is your view?

Write an essay of three or more paragraphs explaining your position on this issue. Support your point of view with specific reasons, facts, or examples. In your essay, use at least two of the words that you have learned in this lesson. Write your essay on a separate sheet of paper.

Unit III Review and Enrichment

 CLOSE READING: Read the following statements. Then answer questions 1–10.

STATEMENTS

Anyone in the seventeenth century who rented a horse from Hobson's stable had to take the one nearest to the door, like it or not.

Dunstan Cass, younger son of the wealthy Squire Cass, broke into Silas Marner's cottage and made off with a bag of gold.

Young David Copperfield could not get along with Mr. Murdstone, his hardhearted stepfather, who made life miserable for him.

Lisa's first words when she came home from the game were: "Is there anything to eat in this house? What's in the refrigerator? When will dinner be ready?"

When Neil Armstrong set foot on the moon on July 20, 1969, he saw nothing but stones, boulders, and craters.

In the first act of *Romeo and Juliet,* peace officers armed with clubs break up a fight between the Montagues and the Capulets on the streets of Verona.

Since the storm was moving rapidly up the coast, the authorities urged residents in low-lying areas to evacuate promptly to higher ground.

As a pioneer on the Dakota prairie, Per Hansa faced many hardships, but he was very enthusiastic about living there.

The strangers decided to go for a swim in the rough surf, scoffing at a sign on the beach that warned, "No lifeguards on duty."

When Terry left her office after work, the winds that had blown so violently in the morning had to her surprise become quite gentle.

QUESTIONS

1. Who seemed ravenous? _____

2. Who took part in a fracas? _____

3. Who appropriated something? _____

4. Who gave no options? _____

5. Who were judged to be vulnerable? _____

6. Who had to put up with someone uncongenial? _____

7. Who noticed a slackening? _____

8. Who showed zeal for something? _____

9. Who defiantly put themselves in jeopardy? _____

10. Who explored an apparently barren place? _____

CONCISE WRITING: Cut the following 180-word editorial to no more than 130 words, without discarding any of its ideas.

The water supply problem has many of our city officials in a state of uncertainty as to what to do. No sooner does one water emergency pass than another seems about to occur. The problem is obviously one that requires immediate attention. Yet some politicians, especially those who like to put off what has to be done to some indefinite time in the future, try to make the problem seem as unimportant as possible. They argue that it will probably solve itself and that we should do nothing about it. But that seems completely contrary to all reason and common sense. We must not wait until our reservoirs are completely empty before taking action. Do we want to go through the same very difficult and trying experiences that many water-starved communities are now suffering?

One promising idea that is now being considered in other places is to speed up the process of installing water meters in every apartment and home. If they have to pay for their water, those people who are now very generous in its use may change their ways.

CLOSE READING: Read the following statements. Then answer questions 11–20.

STATEMENTS

In 1941, two years after negotiating a nonaggression treaty with Stalin, Hitler launched a massive surprise offensive against the Soviet Union.

"This is the last you will see of me," said the customer, storming out the door. "I will never shop here again."

Though the Etruscans controlled much of Italy for centuries before the Romans appeared, no one knows where they and their strange language came from.

After losing her title, the ex-champion was too depressed to talk with reporters.

In 1626, Peter Minuit gave the Native Americans who lived in Manhattan the equivalent of $24 in trinkets for the title to their property.

With the score tied at 2–2, the umpires called the opening game after six innings because of rain.

In *The Deserted Village*, Oliver Goldsmith wrote: "In arguing, too, the parson showed his skill, For even though vanquished, he could argue still."

Tenants returning from shopping were surprised to find that the elevators were not running.

If the Royals had played without Stella, they would not have been able to win.

The new executive saved the company many millions by eliminating wasteful practices.

QUESTIONS

11. Who provided frugal management?_____

12. Who did not anticipate a mechanical breakdown? _____

13. Who was irate? _____

14. Who received seemingly paltry compensation?_____

15. Who broke a pact?_____

16. Who was melancholy? _____

17. Who seemed opinionated? _____

18. Who was indispensable? _____

19. Who curtailed something? _____

20. Who are an enigma? _____

 ANALOGIES: Which lettered pair of words—a, b, c, d, or e—most nearly has the same relationship as the numbered pair? Enter the letter of your answer in the space provided.

1. PICAYUNE : INVALUABLE
   a. steep : sheer
   c. expedient : advisable
   e. trite : fresh
   b. final : conclusive
   d. opportune : favorable
   1. _____

2. HUMANE : MALICE
   a. energetic : vigor
   c. timid : misgiving
   e. appreciative : gratitude
   b. zealous : enthusiasm
   d. unprejudiced : bias
   2. _____

3. DISPARAGE : PRAISE
   a. rue : deplore
   c. deplete : replace
   e. verify : substantiate
   b. prohibit : interdict
   d. mar : impair
   3. _____

4. EFFICIENT : EXPEDITE
   a. greedy : share
   c. dissenting : agree
   e. proficient : botch
   b. gossipy : advertise
   d. thrifty : waste
   4. _____

5. REPAST : HUNGER
   a. infection : fever
   c. nap : fatigue
   e. uncertainty : anxiety
   b. increment : salary
   d. ordeal : tension
   5. _____

VOCABULARY SKILL BUILDER

1. Explain how you can use context clues and your own knowledge and experience to figure out the meaning of each underlined word. Write your answers on a separate sheet of paper.

   a. Having won their eleventh straight game, the players were in a <u>festive</u> mood.

   b. The <u>tension</u> of having to study for three tests given on the same day made me a nervous wreck.

   c. Year after year, Mrs. Ebal deposited $10 a week in the bank. Over time, she <u>amassed</u> well over $10,000.

2. Circle the prefix and/or suffix in each of the following words. Then use the word in a sentence.

   disprove   tactful   untighten

3. Explain the difference between connotation and denotation. Include at least one example in your explanation.

Cumulative Review for Units I, II, and III

A Circle the word that best completes each sentence.

1. Scratches _____ the surface of the wooden table.

   a. expedited   b. marred   c. unnerved   d. wilted

2. Many people pleaded with Senator Torres to run for governor, but she was _____ that she would not.

   a. laborious   b. delectable   c. adamant   d. affluent

3. Cameras were installed around the shopping mall for the purpose of _____.

   a. surveillance   b. stamina   c. enigma   d. conjecture

4. This is not the worst restaurant I've ever eaten in, but it's far from the best. The food is just _____.

   a. mediocre   b. ravenous   c. inclement   d. unkempt

5. Knowing that his girlfriend would be away all summer left Josh in a _____ mood.

   a. melancholy   b. meritorious   c. frugal   d. tactful

6. If you _____ in playing the drums at 7:00 in the morning, I will have to call the police.

   a. persist   b. linger   c. deter   d. convert

7. Drivers who operate a vehicle while talking on a cell phone _____ their own lives and their passengers' lives as well.

   a. infer   b. sustain   c. deplete   d. jeopardize

8. Every citizen has an _____ to vote.

   a. increment   b. iota   c. extraction   d. obligation

9. Detectives searched the countryside for the _____ criminal.

   a. dispensable   b. opportune   c. vulnerable   d. notorious

10. _____ citizens protested the mayor's plan to raise taxes.

    a. Proficient   b. Irate   c. Humane   d. Timid

B Circle the correct synonym for each underlined word.

11. government warnings about a <u>toxic</u> chemical
    a. judicious   b. preeminent   c. poisonous   d. voracious

12. <u>eliminate</u> unnecessary expenses
    a. encroach   b. taunt   c. remove   d. hinder

13. a <u>knack</u> for fixing things
    a. trek   b. tyro   c. talent   d. wharf

14. <u>legible</u> print
    a. viable   b. outmoded   c. fancy   d. readable

15. a <u>lackluster</u> performance
    a. nonessential   b. harsh   c. reprehensible   d. uninspired

16. a character <u>flaw</u>
    a. relic   b. defect   c. inquiry   d. role

17. a <u>feasible</u> plan
    a. viable   b. loquacious   c. prodigious   d. tractable

18. the <u>omnipotent</u> Roman gods
    a. all-powerful   b. impertinent   c. immense   d. threatening

19. <u>vivid</u> details
    a. futile   b. sterile   c. lively   d. prodigal

20. a <u>dearth</u> of rain
    a. surplus   b. countenance   c. bit   d. lack

Vocabulary Index

bold type = lesson word; light type = synonym

Pronunciation Symbols

The system of indicating pronunciation is used by permission. From *Merriam-Webster's Collegiate Dictionary*, Tenth Edition, © 1993 by Merriam-Webster, Incorporated.

ə	banana, collide, abut
'ə, ˌə	humdrum, abut
ᵊ	immediately preceding \l\, \n\, \m\, \ŋ\, as in batt**le**, mitt**en**, eat**en**, and sometimes cap **and** bells \-ᵊm-\ ˡᵒᶜᵏ **and** key \-ᵊŋ-\; immediately following \l\, \m\, \r\, as often in French tab**le**, pris**me**, tit**re**
ər	op**er**ation, furth**er**, **ur**ger
'ər- 'ə-r	as in two different pronunciations of h**urr**y \'hər-ē, 'hə-rē\
a	m**a**t, m**a**p, m**a**d, **ga**g, sn**a**p, p**a**tch
ā	d**ay**, f**a**de, d**a**te, **a**orta, dr**a**pe, c**a**pe
ä	b**o**ther, c**o**t, and, with most American speakers, f**a**ther, c**a**rt
ȧ	f**a**ther as pronounced by speakers who do not rhyme it with b**o**ther
au̇	n**ow**, l**ou**d, **ou**t
b	**b**a**b**y, ri**b**
ch	**ch**in, na**t**ure \'nā-chər\ (actually, this sound is \t\ + \sh\)
d	**d**i**d**, a**dd**er
e	b**e**t, b**e**d, p**e**ck
'ē, ˌē	b**ea**t, nos**e**bl**ee**d, **e**venly, **ea**sy
ē	eas**y**, meal**y**
f	**f**i**f**ty, cu**ff**
g	**g**o, bi**g**, **g**ift
h	**h**at, a**h**ead
hw	**wh**ale as pronounced by those who do not have the same pronunciation for both *whale* and *wail*
i	t**i**p, b**a**nish, act**i**ve
ī	s**i**te, s**i**de, b**uy**, tr**i**pe (actually, this sound is \ä\ + \i\, or \ȧ\ + \i\)

j	job, gem, edge, join, judge (actually, this sound is \d\ + \zh\)
k	kin, cook, ache
k̲	German ich, Buch
l	lily, pool
m	murmur, dim, nymph
n	no, own
ⁿ	indicates that a preceding vowel or diphthong is pronounced with the nasal passages open, as in French un bon vin blanc \oeⁿ-bȯⁿ-vaⁿ-bläⁿ\
ŋ	sing \'siŋ\, singer \'siŋ-ər\, finger \'fiŋ-gər\, ink \'iŋk\
ō	bone, know, beau
ȯ	saw, all, gnaw
œ	French boeuf, German Hölle
œ̄	French feu, German Höhle
ȯi	coin, destroy, sawing
p	pepper, lip
r	red, car, rarity
s	source, less
sh	with nothing between, as in shy, mission, machine, special (actually, this is a single sound, not two); with a hyphen between, two sounds as in death's-head \'deths-,hed\
t	tie, attack
th	with nothing between, as in thin, ether (actually, this is a single sound, not two); with a hyphen between, two sounds as in knighthood \'nīt-,hud\
t̲h̲	then, either, this (actually, this is a single sound, not two)
ü	rule, youth, union \'yün-yən\, few \'fyü\
u̇	pull, wood, book, curable \'kyu̇r-ə-bəl\
ue	German füllen, hübsch
u̅e̅	French rue, German fühlen
v	vivid, give
w	we, away; in some words having final \(,)ō\ a variant \ə-w\ occurs before vowels, as in \'fäl-ə-wiŋ\, covered by the variant \ə(-w)\ at the entry word

y   **y**ard, **y**oung, cue \'kyü\, union \'yün-yən\

ʸ   indicates that during the articulation of the sound represented by the preceding character the front of the tongue has substantially the position it has for the articulation of the first sound of *yard*, as in French *digne* \dēnʸ\

yü   **you**th, **u**nion, c**ue**, f**ew**, m**u**te

yu̇   c**u**rable, f**u**ry

z   **z**one, rai**s**e

zh   with nothing between, as in vi**si**on, azure \'azh-ər\ (actually, this is a single sound, not two); with a hyphen between, two sounds as in ga**z**e**h**ound \'gāz-ˌhau̇nd\

\   slant line used in pairs to mark the beginning and end of a transcription: \'pen\

ˈ   mark preceding a syllable with primary (strongest) stress: \'-pen-mən-ˌship\

ˌ   mark preceding a syllable with secondary (next-strongest) stress: \'pen-mən-ˌship\

-     mark of syllable division

( )   indicate that what is symbolized between is present in some utterances but not in others: *factory* \'fak-t(ə)rē\